MADE IN AMERICA

bluestem
the cookbook

colby garrelts and megan garrelts

with bonjwing lee

· MADE IN ·
AMERICA

A MODERN COLLECTION of
CLASSIC RECIPES

COLBY & MEGAN
GARRELTS

PHOTOGRAPHY BY BONJWING LEE

Andrews McMeel
Publishing

Kansas City · Sydney · London

WE DEDICATE THIS BOOK TO

our family

FOR THE RECIPES AND LOVE
PASSED DOWN THROUGH
GENERATIONS.

CONTENTS

ACKNOWLEDGMENTS

We would like to thank the many people in our lives who inspire and support us, making it possible to live our dream.

To our children, whom we love to the moon and back: Madilyn and Colin, thank you for your love, excitement, and curiosity.

To our parents, Bob and Kaye Schultz, Kristie Swearngin, and Greg and Linda Garrelts: You have helped us achieve our goals and encouraged us through our journey.

To our grandparents, whom we miss dearly: Thank you for the traditions and recipes passed down.

To our restaurant families at Bluestem and Rye: Thank you for creating amazing meals with us! Thanks to John Brogan, Ryan Williams, Andrew Longres, Kevin Dold, Nate Mouzoukos, Sam Diagle, Kelly Conwell, Jessica Armstrong, Tim Veith, Jeremy Lamb, Eric Willey, Van Zarr, Jeff Cambiano, Jennifer Young, and Susan Kane.

To Jeff and Joy Stehney: Thank you for sharing your love for American cooking with us and for your support and mentorship that has helped us on our journey.

To Bonjwing Lee: Thank you for incredible photographs and countless moments eating, tasting, and dining together.

To Susan Champlin, our writer, who helped us bring this book together: Thank you for your careful editing and attention to detail.

To our editor, Jean Lucas, and her team at Andrews McMeel: Thank you for believing in us.

To Jane Dystel: Thank you for your great spirit and kind words.

To Jamie Estes and Tammie Franck: Thank you for sharing our story.

To Louise Meyers and her incredible shop, Pryde's Old Westport: Thank you for all your support through the years and for your incredible kitchen supply collection!

To the farmers and our fellow K.C. craftsmen: Thank you for providing us with amazing ingredients.

To our patrons and guests who celebrate their lives with us around our tables at the restaurants, we are forever grateful.

To our colleagues in Kansas City and beyond who live to cook and cook to live.

Finally, thanks to every mom-and-pop, small, roadside diner, and to little nooks across America that we ate in and traveled through from childhood to present—those special moments have molded how we eat and what we love about American cooking.

A SHOT TO THE "MID" SECTION

Megan and Colby Garrelts possess a unique quality, one that is all the more glaring as each day passes. They deeply understand the essence of food and the experience dining should be. And though their food and restaurants are outstanding, it is their ability to see to the core of that food and the greater implications of the dining experience that I fell for. They truly adore what they do and are able to telegraph that message through all facets of the experience at both Bluestem and Rye. Both are places that, in spite of the disparity in their concepts, offer a warmth and welcome that most restaurants never approach.

It was precisely this that drew me to the Garrelts and exactly why I fell so deeply in love with Kansas City the very first time I visited. It is a unique place that a particularly ethnocentric Southerner found appealing: In spite of the fact that he may have felt that the hospitality of the South was entirely unparalleled, this Southerner was massively surprised and pleased to find that it extended north beyond Kentucky and west beyond Louisiana . . . maybe (sorry, Texas, the jury's still out).

When we met, Megan and Colby were struggling with the same thing a number of chefs in our corner of the industry wrestle with. It is an emergence from what I call the "creative hibernation" that comes at the beginning of our careers. We tend, as ambitious youngsters, to dive into the deep end of the pool, feeling we need to dazzle people with creative presentations, challenge our guests with previously unimagined combinations, and, God forbid, confuse/surprise the same folks with altered molecular structure of our food.

There comes a moment, though, for most chefs, when you realize that while quality, technique, and ambition are important, you never truly excel until you realize that you are cooking for your guests's experience and not for your self-absorbed personal expression. Cooking is about making people happy. It is about transporting them to a place they can escape the day's troubles, a place that reminds them of enjoyable times, a place they can celebrate important moments.

The food in these pages is the journey to that understanding. These are recipes that illustrate where the food of the Midwest is in this moment. It draws a picture of a place's history, whether by nodding to European immigrants who settled here or giving a big ol' bear hug to the cattle industry on which so much prosperity was built.

So, dive in. Taste of mid-America. These guys have provided a roadmap to delightful cooking and satisfying eating. I count the minutes until I can return. In the meantime, I have this book.

★ INTRODUCTION ★

For a country that's famous for its amber waves of grain, the landscape of American food is amazingly diverse and colorful, woven with the flavors of every culture that has added to our collective heritage. The Native Americans knew the land best—they identified every nut, grain, and seed, every berry fruit, freshwater fish, and type of wild game. They hunted and foraged not for culinary achievement but for nourishment and survival. New arrivals from all corners of the world came to America, bringing the languages, cultures, and flavors of their homelands, while discovering a land of plenty around them.

Today, American roadways once carved by pioneers are lined with rustic roadhouses, classic diners, and rural restaurants that highlight the renowned foods in each region—from fried chicken stands to barbecue joints, from delis to crab shacks, and in bakeshops everywhere that celebrate the all-American slice of pie. At home, American traditions embrace both history and family, in classic Thanksgiving feasts and picnics on quilts under a night sky filled with fireworks on our nation's birthday.

The food of the Midwest is the last untold tale in modern American cooking, but it's a central one—in every sense of the word. In the nineteenth century, farmland in the middle of the country was cheap, attracting thousands who hoped to make their living off the land. For others, the Midwest was the last stop

before the arduous journey west. Some travelers kept going, but others stayed put, and their traditions and recipes took root with them.

For us, the roots of our love for food and cooking, the inspiration for becoming chefs—and really, a big part of the reason we were drawn to each other!—reach back to our own family tables: Five generations of Colby's in Kansas and Megan's in Illinois. Born and bred in the middle of America, we share the same memories of fresh corn off the stalk in hot summers, slow-cooked meats, and handmade sweets that filled our grandmas' homes.

The recurring theme in this book is *family*: Cooking in America is profoundly based on tradition, and here in the middle, recipes are shared among families, passed along through a "potluck" of cards tucked into a tin box or just by watching your grandmother at work in the kitchen. You pick up a recipe box to make pies, and you know the recipe for pickling garden vegetables by heart.

In this cookbook, we share our simple approach to food and cooking—the kind of cooking we do in our own kitchen at home. Our lives here are always tied into the seasons, to what's growing in our gardens, to what's sizzling on the grill on hot summer nights, and to what's simmering on the stovetop during frigid winter days.

Breakfast is substantial in the Midwest—it has to fuel the farmers who work the land—so you'll find Biscuits and Gravy (page 8) and German Apple Pancakes (page 7) among other hearty ways to start your day. When the weather's good, we can head outside and fire up the grill, cooking what Colby will tell you is some of the most versatile—and, of course, the best—barbecue in the country. His recipe for Pulled Pork Sandwiches (page 82) is an example of true Kansas City barbecue. Of course, no one in Kansas City can have a pantry without a sauce for barbecue or meat off the grill, and the BBQ, Steak, and Hot Sauces (pages 26–29) are our modern renditions of traditional American table sauces.

Cooler (or downright cold) months in Kansas are a reason to move inside and start cooking with cast iron or in the Dutch oven. That's when dishes like Madeira-Braised Chicken with Sour Cherries (page 51) and Slow-Cooked Pale Ale Barley (page 53) will warm the kitchen and your soul. And any cookbook claiming to celebrate American traditions must include a recipe for fried chicken; on page 91 you'll find the recipe we make at our restaurant Rye in Leawood, Kansas, where we serve over a ton of fried chicken a week to our loyal guests.

A meal in America—whether at Grandma's house, at the church potluck, or at any celebration anywhere—isn't over until you've enjoyed something homespun and sweet. Megan's Banana Cream Pie (page 116) is an American classic—the blend of butter and lard in the piecrust is a nod to the days when lard was more commonly used and butter was a luxury. The Corn Cookies with Milk Jam and Strawberries (page 128) is a simple combination with roots in the original johnnycake.

Finally, we offer a series of menus to help you celebrate some major American holidays and important family events (see page 144).

"Give the people what they want" is a phrase we used a lot when creating Rye, our restaurant showcasing the food and flavors of the Midwest. In this book, we intend to do the same: offer humble recipes, stories from around our table, and a new perspective on what it means to be from the middle in terms of how we cook, eat, and live.

ONE

Daybreak

In our home, we believe that sharing a warm, homemade breakfast is the perfect way to start the day with the people you love. I remember my father and brother taking turns making Sunday morning brunch for my mom and me; banana bread, pancakes, and cheesy scrambled eggs always graced our table. Colby spent Saturday mornings watching cartoons on a small black-and-white TV set in the kitchen while his sister whipped up a batch of French toast. The nice thing about breakfast recipes is that they do not intimidate—even a kitchen novice will tackle an egg to cook a morning meal.

The recipes in this chapter offer our favorite sweet and savory selections for building your own special morning: classics like German Apple Pancakes (page 7) and Biscuits and Gravy (page 8), along with our new takes on old favorites, like Corn Fritters with Fresh Sheep's Milk Cheese (page 21) and Chipped Beef on Toast with Cured Beef and Spinach (page 4). Some are quick and easy; others take a little more time and may be reserved for special-occasion brunches. Just add a spicy Bloody Mary (page 17) or a celebratory glass of bubbles to top off the morning and to toast the people who share your kitchen. ★ M.G.

SPICY TOMATO AND BURNT-ENDS HASH
with
FRIED EGGS

S E R V E S   6

This is an egg dish we came up with as a special at Bluestem some years ago. We had a ton of preserved tomatoes that we needed to use up, but that sounded a little boring . . . until we grabbed some burnt ends from our brisket. Now this has become one of the most iconic brunch dishes we offer: It's smoky, spicy, and very satisfying. ★ C.G.

To make the sauce, place the tomatoes, garlic, Worcestershire sauce, hot sauce, and horseradish in a food processor and pulse until the mixture is well chopped but not puréed. Set aside.

To make the hash, heat 2 tablespoons of the canola oil in a large sauté pan over medium heat. Add the sliced potatoes and fry for 6 to 8 minutes, until golden brown; set aside. Using the same sauté pan, heat 3 more tablespoons of the canola oil over medium heat. Add the bell peppers and onion to the hot oil and cook for about 10 minutes, stirring occasionally, until the vegetables are caramelized. Transfer the caramelized vegetables to a medium bowl and reserve.

Using the same sauté pan, heat the remaining 2 tablespoons canola oil over medium heat. Add the brisket burnt ends to the oil and cook for 2 to 3 minutes to brown the burnt ends. Return the fried potatoes and caramelized peppers and onions to the sauté pan and cook for another minute. Add the tomato sauce and stir together to evenly coat the burnt ends and vegetables. Keep warm over low heat while making the eggs.

To make the fried eggs, heat the oil in a 10 to 12-inch skillet over low heat. Crack 2 of the eggs into a bowl and season with salt and pepper. Increase the heat under the skillet to medium-high and add the butter to the skillet. When the butter is melted, add the 2 eggs and cover the skillet with a lid. Cook the eggs for 20 to 30 seconds, until the egg whites are opaque; remove from the pan and reserve on a warm plate. Repeat with the remaining eggs.

To serve, divide the hash among 6 plates and place an egg on top of each. Garnish with minced chives.

SAUCE
- 3 cups canned San Marzano tomatoes, with juice (see Note)
- 5 cloves garlic, peeled
- 2 tablespoons Worcestershire sauce
- 2 tablespoons Hot Sauce (page 28) or store-bought
- 1 tablespoon prepared horseradish

HASH
- 7 tablespoons canola oil
- 2 cups sliced fingerling potatoes or other waxy potato variety, such as Yukon gold
- 2 red bell peppers, sliced ¼ inch thick
- 1 large yellow onion, sliced ⅛ inch thick
- 2 cups cubed Smoked Brisket burnt ends (page 81) or hearty sausage

EGGS
- 4 teaspoons canola oil
- 6 large eggs
- Kosher salt and freshly ground black pepper
- 4 teaspoons unsalted butter
- Minced chives, for garnish

NOTE

If you put up your own tomatoes, feel free to use those in place of the canned tomatoes.

Chipped Beef on Toast
with Cured Beef and Spinach

★ S E R V E S   4 ★

This was one of my childhood favorites. I remember my mom making it when I was very young; I'd eat the salty dried beef straight out of the bag and drive my mother crazy. I hadn't thought about it for years until we were on a visit to relatives one recent summer and my aunt made it again for my kids. I was excited by the nostalgia and the simplicity and by how comforting it was. As I watched my Aunt Karen thicken milk with a slurry of cornstarch and water, I realized that this was a white gravy with sliced cured beef over toast. So I gussied it up with good bresaola (salted and cured beef from northern Italy), paired it with some crusty bread and some vinegary greens, and fell in love with it all over again. ★ C.G.

4 tablespoons (½ stick) unsalted butter

4 slices good-quality French bread

White Gravy (recipe follows)

8 ounces bresaola or other cured beef, sliced

2 tablespoons canola oil

2 cloves garlic, sliced

1 shallot, minced

4 cups loosely packed fresh spinach leaves

1 teaspoon sherry vinegar

Preheat the oven to 425°F. Melt the butter in a small sauce pan. Brush the sliced bread with the butter, place it on a baking sheet, and bake until the bread is golden brown, flipping the bread once during cooking, about 10 minutes.

In a medium sauce pan, gently rewarm the white gravy over medium heat, adding water or milk to loosen as necessary. Stir in the bresaola. Keep warm until ready to serve.

Heat the oil in a medium sauté pan over medium heat. Add the garlic and shallots and cook just until translucent, about 2 minutes. Add the spinach and quickly sauté until just wilted, about 40 seconds. Remove the pan from the heat. Add the vinegar to the wilted spinach and toss.

To serve, place 1 slice of toast on each of 4 plates. Ladle the bresaola and gravy over each toast slice, followed by a spoonful of spinach on top of the sauce, and serve immediately. Any leftover bresaola in gravy may be refrigerated in an airtight container for up to 3 days. The sauce may need a splash of whole milk when being reheated.

Continued

White Gravy **Makes about 5 cups**

Gravy is to Kansas what tomato sauce is to Italy. Add some sausage or chipped beef to this base, and we'll put it on everything: chicken, biscuits, fried steaks, toast, you name it! If you make the base right, everything else is easy. It's best to make the gravy a day ahead and refrigerate it overnight to let the flavors meld. This recipe makes plenty of gravy, so you can serve it alongside any breakfast item—it's the perfect excuse to linger at the kitchen table, talking and dipping. ★ C.G.

8 tablespoons (1 stick) unsalted butter

½ cup minced shallots

4 medium cloves garlic, smashed and minced or pressed through garlic press

⅓ cup plus 2 tablespoons unbleached all-purpose flour

4 cups whole milk

2 dried bay leaves

Kosher salt and freshly ground black pepper

1 cup grated Parmesan cheese

Melt the butter in a medium sauce pan over medium heat until foaming, 3 to 4 minutes. Add the shallots and garlic and cook, stirring frequently, until translucent, about 4 minutes. Add the flour and cook, stirring constantly, until you get a little blond color, about 4 minutes. Gradually whisk in the milk and add the bay leaves. Bring the mixture to a boil over medium-high heat and then lower to a simmer for about 10 minutes. Season to taste with salt and pepper.

Decrease the heat to low and simmer for 10 minutes, or until thickened, whisking occasionally. Whisk in the Parmesan and discard the bay leaves. For best results, let the gravy cool, then refrigerate overnight in an airtight container. Rewarm gently before using, adding a little water or milk to loosen as necessary.

GERMAN APPLE PANCAKES

When I was growing up in suburban Chicago, pancake houses and German restaurants were familiar stops on our eating-out trips. My family often enjoyed going with Grandma and Grandpa Schultz to our neighborhood pancake house, where we devoured Dutch babies and German pancakes. This recipe is my version of the traditional hearty breakfast we once shared. Buttermilk and orange juice give a touch of extra tartness to the mix, but you can substitute apple cider for the orange juice to add another layer of apple flavor. For a sweeter topping, use soft whipped cream with a pinch of cinnamon sugar. ★ M.G.

¾ cup unbleached all-purpose flour

¾ cup buttermilk

3 large eggs

½ teaspoon kosher salt

4 tablespoons (½ stick) unsalted butter

¼ cup firmly packed light brown sugar

3 tart apples (such as Granny Smith), peeled, cored, and sliced

⅔ cup freshly squeezed orange juice

½ teaspoon ground cinnamon

½ cup sour cream

Confectioners' sugar, for dusting

Preheat the oven to 400°F. Combine the flour, buttermilk, eggs, and salt in a blender. Blend on high speed for about 1 minute or until the mixture is thoroughly combined; set the batter aside.

In an 8 to 10-inch ovenproof nonstick skillet over medium heat, heat the butter and brown sugar until the butter is melted. Add the apples, orange juice, and cinnamon to the butter and brown sugar and cook until the apples become tender and translucent and the orange juice reduces to a thick syrup, about 12 minutes.

Pour the pancake batter into the apple skillet and use a spatula to swirl the batter and apples together. Transfer the skillet to the oven and bake the pancake for 10 to 12 minutes, until the pancake puffs up slightly in the center and is cooked through (a tester inserted in the center will come out clean). Turn the hot pancake out onto a serving platter and slice into wedges.

To serve, place a dollop of sour cream in the center of each slice and dust with confectioners' sugar. Serve immediately.

BISCUITS and GRAVY

★ ★ ★ ★ ★ ★

SERVES 6
(MAKES 12 BISCUITS)

BISCUITS

2 cups unbleached all-purpose flour

1 tablespoon baking powder

1 teaspoon sugar

½ teaspoon kosher salt

8 tablespoons (1 stick) cold unsalted butter, cubed

1¼ cups buttermilk, plus more for brushing

SAUSAGE GRAVY

1½ pounds ground pork

1 tablespoon kosher salt

1 tablespoon chopped fresh flat-leaf parsley

1 tablespoon chopped fresh thyme

1 tablespoon chopped fresh sage

2 cloves garlic, minced

1 tablespoon orange zest

2 tablespoons plus 1 teaspoon chicken stock

1 tablespoon sherry vinegar

2 tablespoons vegetable oil

1 small yellow onion, diced

White Gravy (page 6)

A staple in the Midwest, biscuits and gravy are a hearty breakfast tradition. You can give the dish a unique hometown flavor by sourcing ground pork from your favorite local butcher; or if you don't have the time for homemade sausage, use your favorite purchased country sausage. You can also use this sausage recipe for our Christmas Casserole (page 19). Bake the biscuits the same day you want to eat them, and serve them warm, with the gravy dripping over the top. ★ C.G., M.G.

To make the biscuits, position a rack in the center of the oven and preheat to 350°F. Line a baking sheet with parchment paper and set aside.

In a food processor, combine the flour, baking powder, sugar, and salt; pulse to combine. Add the cold butter in thirds, pulsing several times after each addition until the mixture resembles coarse meal. Slowly add the buttermilk, pulsing just until a dough forms.

Turn the dough out onto a floured work surface. Working quickly, knead the dough just until all the buttermilk is distributed and the dough looks smooth. Roll the biscuit dough out to a ½-inch thickness and cut out the biscuits using a 3-inch round biscuit cutter. Transfer the biscuits to the prepared baking sheet and lightly brush the tops with more buttermilk. Bake for 15 to 20 minutes, until golden brown.

To make the sausage gravy, place the pork and salt in the bowl of a stand mixer fitted with the paddle attachment. Using a large mortar and pestle, mash the parsley, thyme, sage, garlic, and orange zest with the stock and vinegar to form a paste; if you have a small blender, that will work, too. Mix the pork in the stand mixer for 2 minutes. Add the herb mixture and mix for another 3 minutes.

In a large cast-iron skillet over medium-high heat, heat the oil until it shimmers, about 2 minutes. Add the diced onion and cook for 2 minutes, or until slightly translucent. Stir in the sausage and crumble with a wooden spoon. Cook until the sausage starts to crisp slightly, 6 to 7 minutes. Drain the fat and place the sausage on a plate lined with a paper towel.

In a medium sauce pan, gently rewarm the White Gravy over medium heat, adding water or milk to loosen as necessary. Add the sausage to the gravy and keep warm until ready to serve.

To serve, place 2 whole biscuits on each plate and ladle the sausage gravy over the top (reserve excess gravy for dipping breakfast sides). Serve immediately.

BLUEBERRY-OAT BREAKFAST CAKE

MAKES ONE 8-INCH SQUARE CAKE

I love a morning cake that features fresh berries or fruit, especially in the summertime—a cake that comes out of the oven overflowing with fruit, so that you just have to eat it straight from the pan. This is that cake. We often assemble these cakes in individual ramekins the night before a busy Sunday morning brunch at the restaurants. You can do the same thing after assembling the batter, blueberries, and streusel in the cake pan; just keep it covered in the refrigerator overnight, and bake it in the morning. But once you bake it, this cake is best eaten the same day, with a dollop of cream. ★ M.G.

OAT STREUSEL

¾ cup firmly packed light brown sugar

4 tablespoons (½ stick) cold unsalted butter

¼ cup unbleached all-purpose flour

½ teaspoon ground cinnamon

⅛ teaspoon kosher salt

½ cup old-fashioned rolled oats

CAKE

¾ cup granulated sugar

8 tablespoons (1 stick) unsalted butter, softened

Finely grated zest of 1 lemon

2 large eggs

2 tablespoons buttermilk

2 teaspoons pure vanilla extract

1⅛ cups unbleached all-purpose flour

2 teaspoons baking powder

½ teaspoon kosher salt

2 pints fresh blueberries

Confectioners' sugar, for dusting

1 cup heavy cream, whipped to soft peaks, for serving

To make the oat streusel, place the brown sugar, butter, flour, cinnamon, and salt in a food processor. Pulse until the mixture resembles coarse meal. Transfer the streusel mixture to a medium bowl and gently fold in the oats. Set aside in the refrigerator. (You may transfer the streusel to an airtight container or resealable plastic bag and freeze for up to 1 month.)

To make the cake, preheat the oven to 350°F. Grease an 8-inch square cake pan and set aside.

Combine the sugar, butter, and lemon zest in the bowl of a stand mixer fitted with the paddle attachment. Cream the mixture until light and fluffy, 6 to 8 minutes. Add the eggs, buttermilk, and vanilla to the creamed butter mixture and mix to combine.

In a small bowl, whisk together the flour, baking powder, and salt. Add the dry ingredients to the butter mixture and mix until just incorporated, making sure to scrape down the sides of the bowl while mixing. Transfer the cake batter to the prepared cake pan, using a spatula to spread the cake batter evenly. Once the batter is evenly spread across the bottom of the cake pan, use the spatula to smear the batter up the sides of the pan, coating the entire inside of the cake pan. Spread the blueberries across the top of the cake batter, then sprinkle the oat streusel topping evenly over the blueberries to cover. (The cake can be prepared to this point and refrigerated, covered, overnight.)

Bake the cake until it is golden brown along the edges and the center begins to bubble from the blueberries, about 45 minutes. Let cool to room temperature before slicing into wedges; the cake will sink slightly in the center from the weight of the berries. Serve at room temperature or warm slightly before serving, topping each slice with a dusting of confectioners' sugar and a dollop of freshly whipped cream.

FRIED CINNAMON ROLLS

MAKES 24 MINI ROLLS OR 12 LARGE ROLLS

Freshly baked cinnamon rolls—with their yeast-raised dough, butter-and-cinnamon smear, and sweet, gooey icing—are among my favorite items to come out of a bakeshop. Cinnamon rolls are also perfect for little hands to help with. My children will often take turns helping me roll the dough and spread the smear, and my son loves to punch down the dough. In this recipe, we prepare the dough and then fry the rolls to finish, giving them a deliciously crisp crust with a soft and tender interior. The mini rolls are better for frying, but if you prefer to make large rolls and bake them for a traditional presentation, I've included those instructions as well. ★ M.G.

ROLLS

3½ cups unbleached all-purpose flour, plus more for dusting and kneading

¼ cup plus 2 tablespoons granulated sugar

1 tablespoon instant dry yeast

1¼ teaspoons kosher salt

1 cup whole milk

5 tablespoons unsalted butter

3 large eggs, at room temperature

CINNAMON SMEAR

5 tablespoons unsalted butter, softened

⅓ cup firmly packed light brown sugar

¼ cup honey

1 tablespoon ground cinnamon

ICING

¾ cup confectioners' sugar

¼ cup heavy cream

2 tablespoons unsalted butter, softened

1 teaspoon pure vanilla extract

Canola oil, for frying

To make the rolls, grease a large bowl. Have a clean, dry towel handy; set aside. Place the flour, granulated sugar, yeast, and salt in a stand mixer fitted with the paddle attachment. Mix on low speed to combine the dry ingredients, about 1 minute. Place the milk and the butter in a small microwaveable bowl and heat in the microwave on low power for about 45 seconds to warm the milk and melt the butter. In a medium bowl, beat the eggs, then whisk in the warmed milk and melted butter mixture. Add the liquid ingredients to the dry ingredients and mix on low speed until the dough becomes soft and sticky and pulls from the sides of the bowl, about 4 minutes.

Remove the paddle attachment and replace it with a dough hook. Continue to mix the dough on low speed for 2 minutes. Stop the mixer and use a sturdy spatula to give the bowl one final scrape. Dust the top of the dough lightly with flour. Continue to mix for 4 minutes on medium speed, until the sticky mass becomes smooth and springs back at the touch. If needed, dust the dough again with flour while mixing to prevent sticking. Place the dough in the greased bowl and cover with the dry towel. Put the bowl in a warm place until the dough doubles in size, about 2 hours.

Meanwhile, make the cinnamon smear. Place the butter, brown sugar, honey, and cinnamon in a stand mixer fitted with the paddle attachment. Mix the ingredients together, scraping the bowl to fully incorporate, about 3 minutes.

Continued

Lightly flour a work surface. Once the dough has doubled in size, punch it down and transfer to the floured surface. Roll the dough out to a ¼-inch-thick rectangle measuring about 6 by 24 inches. Spread the smear evenly over the rolled dough, leaving about ½ inch of the dough as an edge. Starting from one long side of the rectangle, roll the dough to form a tight cylinder. Slice the dough into 24 mini rolls or 12 large rolls and transfer to a nonstick baking sheet. Put the baking sheet in a warm place until the rolls have doubled again in size, 30 to 40 minutes.

Meanwhile, make the icing. In a small bowl, whisk together the confectioners' sugar, cream, butter, and vanilla. Set aside until ready to use.

Once the rolls have doubled in size, insert 2 toothpicks horizontally through each mini roll to secure the ends before frying. Fill a large deep sauté pan halfway with the oil and heat over medium heat. A home fryer may also be used to fry the cinnamon rolls, using canola oil to fill the oil chamber to the manufacturer's recommended fill line and heating the fryer to 350°F.

Using tongs, carefully drop the cinnamon rolls into the hot oil, 3 at a time. Fry the cinnamon rolls for 2 to 3 minutes on each side, until golden brown. Transfer the rolls to a plate lined with paper towels to drain. Repeat the process with the remaining rolls. (Alternatively, the cinnamon rolls can be baked rather than fried. After the sliced rolls go through the second rising, transfer the rolls to an 8 by 12-inch greased baking pan with a rim—no need to skewer them with toothpicks—and bake at 350°F for 15 to 20 minutes, until golden brown.)

Once they are all fried or baked, transfer the warm rolls to a serving platter and drizzle with the icing. Serve immediately.

BAKED OATMEAL *WITH* SORGHUM

Serves 6

My son loves oatmeal, and my wife will often choose it as her late-night snack—we are a breakfast family. Almost every day there is some variation of oatmeal prepared in our home, but this recipe is very special: It's rich, sweet, and a perfect start for a snowy day. Leftovers will keep, refrigerated, for 1 day. To reheat, pour a little milk or cream over the top and heat, covered, in a 325°F oven for 8 to 10 minutes. Note: Sorghum is commonly found in Midwest and southern cooking. It is a sweetener made from grain and used like honey or molasses; it has a buttery flavor note, however, and is not as intense as a molasses-style syrup. ★ C.G.

TOPPING

1 cup dried cherries

1 cup raisins

1 cup bourbon or apple cider

½ cup honey

OATMEAL

2 cups old-fashioned rolled oats

¼ cup chopped pecans, toasted

¼ cup sliced almonds, toasted

1½ teaspoons ground cinnamon

1 teaspoon baking powder

½ teaspoon fine sea salt

1 cup whole milk

1 cup heavy cream

⅓ cup sorghum

1 large egg

1 tablespoon plus 1 teaspoon unsalted butter, melted

2 teaspoons pure vanilla extract

Softly whipped cream, for serving

To make the topping, soak the cherries and raisins in the bourbon for 1 hour.

Drain any excess liquid and toss the cherries and raisins with the honey. Set aside until ready to use.

Preheat the oven to 375°F. Butter an 8-inch square baking dish.

To make the oatmeal, in a medium bowl, mix together the oats, pecans, almonds, cinnamon, baking powder, and salt. In another medium bowl, whisk together the milk, cream, sorghum, egg, butter, and vanilla. Place the oat-nut mixture in the baking dish and pour the liquid ingredients over the top. Let stand for 10 minutes to ensure that the liquid has integrated with the oat mixture. Top with the cherry-raisin mixture and bake for 45 minutes, or until golden brown. Serve hot, with a dollop of softly whipped cream.

COUNTRY GRANOLA

★ MAKES 10 CUPS ★

Just as my son loves oatmeal, I love granola—the crunch, the nuts, the fruit. Used as a topping for yogurt, sprinkled on fruit, enjoyed with milk, or simply eaten by the handful, this treat is always available in the pantry at our home or in the restaurants. Granola is also one of the most versatile breakfast snacks in the kitchen: You can use whatever kinds of nuts and dried fruit you prefer. This granola keeps for up to 5 days in an airtight container at room temperature. ★ C.G.

2 egg whites

6 cups old-fashioned rolled oats

1½ cups sunflower seeds

1½ cups walnut pieces

1 cup dried cranberries

1 cup firmly packed light brown sugar

1 cup dark corn syrup

½ cup olive oil

1½ teaspoons kosher salt

1 teaspoon ground cinnamon

Preheat the oven to 325°F. Lightly grease a rimmed baking sheet.

In a large bowl, whisk the egg whites until frothy. Add the oats, sunflower seeds, walnuts, cranberries, brown sugar, corn syrup, olive oil, salt, and cinnamon to the frothy egg whites and stir well with a wooden spoon to evenly combine. Transfer the granola mixture to the prepared baking sheet, making sure to spread the granola evenly over the entire pan. Bake the granola for 8 minutes, then use a wooden spoon to gently stir the hot granola to ensure even baking. Rotate the pan and bake for another 8 minutes, or until the nuts and oats are thoroughly toasted and the corn syrup begins to bubble.

Let cool completely. With a spatula, transfer the baked granola to a storage container. Make sure that the granola has cooled completely before covering the container, so as not to seal in any steam; otherwise the granola will get soggy.

Bloody Mary

BLOODY MARY MIX

2 cups good-quality canned tomatoes, such as San Marzano, with juice

½ cup Hot Sauce (page 28)

¼ cup BBQ Sauce (page 26)

2½ tablespoons prepared horseradish

1½ tablespoons Worcestershire sauce

10 cloves garlic, smashed

3 shallots, diced

2½ tablespoons freshly squeezed lemon juice

2½ tablespoons distilled white vinegar

1 teaspoon celery salt

½ teaspoon kosher salt

SERVING

Celery salt (¼ teaspoon per serving)

Lemon or lime, sliced, for rimming the glass

Vodka, such as Tito's (1½ ounces per serving)

Ice cubes

Quick Pickles, page 37

Other garnishes: pickled pearl onions, cherry peppers, blue cheese–stuffed olives, bacon pieces, celery sticks

To make the mix, place the tomatoes, hot sauce, barbecue sauce, horseradish, Worcestershire sauce, garlic, shallots, lemon juice, vinegar, celery salt, and kosher salt in a blender. Blend on high speed until the mixture is smooth. Transfer the mixture to an airtight container and refrigerate until ready to use, up to 1 week.

To serve, rim a pint glass with ¼ teaspoon celery salt. Place the salt on a shallow plate, run a sliced lime or lemon around the rim, and gently dip the glass rim into the salt, turning the glass in one direction until the rim is completely coated in a thin layer of salt. Add 1½ ounces of vodka to the glass and fill three-fourths of the glass with Bloody Mary mix, then top with ice. Stir together, add a celery stick, and top with desired garnish(es).

Christmas Day brings a morning of traditions to our home. Our children, Madilyn and Colin, scamper around the tree in their pj's, and after all of our gifts are unwrapped, we sit down to eat. Fortunately, everything is ready to go, because on Christmas Eve I set our kitchen table for our fancy morning brunch and prepare this casserole in advance. This recipe is very forgiving and allows for additional vegetables to be added—green peppers, tomatoes, celery, or whatever you like. And since it can be prepared the night before, you can relax and enjoy your own Christmas morning traditions. ★ M.G.

3 cups croutons, preferably brioche croutons

1 pound uncooked sausage (page 8)

½ cup sliced cremini mushrooms (optional)

¼ cup diced yellow onion

1 cup shredded sharp cheddar cheese

1 cup shredded Gruyère cheese

2 tablespoons chopped fresh flat-leaf parsley

2½ cups whole milk

1¼ cups White Gravy (page 6) or 1 (10.75-ounce) can cream of mushroom soup

4 large eggs

¼ teaspoon kosher salt

Freshly ground black pepper

Christmas CASSEROLE

Preheat the oven to 350°F. Grease an 8 by 12-inch baking pan.

Distribute the croutons evenly in the pan. Top the croutons with the sausage, then the mushrooms (if using), onions, cheddar, and Gruyère. Sprinkle the parsley all over the top. In a medium bowl, whisk the milk, White Gravy, eggs, salt, and a few turns of pepper to combine. Pour the mixture over the casserole ingredients in the pan. (The casserole can be prepared to this point, covered, and refrigerated overnight, if desired.)

Bake the casserole for 1 hour or until the sausage begins to bubble and brown and the eggs soufflé to the top of the pan. Allow the casserole to cool slightly, and serve warm. Any leftovers can be covered and refrigerated for up to 3 days; the casserole is delicious reheated for 2 or 3 minutes in the microwave.

Corn Fritters
with Fresh Sheep's Milk Cheese

★ **MAKES 14 FRITTERS** ★

Nothing warms a breakfast table more than a bowl of warm cornmeal fritters. Here in the Midwest, corn is abundant and used in many forms in both sweet and savory recipes. These fritters are slightly sweet, and we pair them with a creamy, fresh sheep's milk cheese from our local Green Dirt Farm in Weston, Missouri. You can use your favorite soft cheese to dip the warm fritters in, or any cheese with a texture similar to ricotta. Yogurt or sour cream would also make a nice dipping side, or, in the summer, a tangy green tomato jam. ★ **M.G.**

½ cup yellow cornmeal
½ cup unbleached all-purpose flour
¼ cup sugar
½ teaspoon kosher salt
¼ teaspoon baking soda
1 large egg, beaten
½ cup buttermilk
¼ cup sliced scallions
Canola oil, for frying
1 cup fresh sheep's milk cheese
    or ricotta

In a medium bowl, mix together the cornmeal, flour, sugar, salt, and baking soda. Make a well in the center and add the egg and the buttermilk, mixing gently for about 8 strokes, being careful not to overmix. Fold the scallions into the batter.

Fill a large, deep sauté pan halfway with the oil and heat over medium heat. A home fryer may also be used to fry the fritters, using canola oil to fill the oil chamber to the manufacturer's recommended fill line and heating the fryer to 350°F.

Using 2 tablespoons, carefully add dollops of the cornmeal batter to the hot oil, about 4 at a time. Fry the fritters for 2 to 3 minutes on each side, until golden brown. Drain on a plate lined with paper towels. Repeat until the batter is all used.

To serve, place the warm fritters in a basket or serving bowl and serve with a bowl of fresh sheep's milk cheese alongside.

BRAISED BACON WITH BOURBON RAISINS, NUTS, AND FRIED EGGS

SERVES 4

I love to take traditional dishes and turn them on their head, and this is a great way to rethink bacon and eggs. The braise and broth are satisfying and delicious—perfect on a winter's day—but the bacon is certainly the star of this show. I know the quantity of bacon looks like a lot, but don't worry! It will drastically shrink. ★ C.G.

BACON

- 3 pounds unsliced slab bacon, scored and divided into 4 portions
- 1 medium yellow onion, chopped
- 5 cloves garlic, chopped
- 1/3 cup firmly packed light brown sugar
- 1 cup dry white wine
- 1 cup stout beer
- 1 cup apple cider
- 4 cups chicken stock
- 2 large sprigs oregano

TOPPING

- 1 cup raisins
- 1/2 cup bourbon
- 1/4 cup sliced almonds
- 1/4 cup pecans, roughly chopped
- 1/4 cup sunflower seeds
- 1/4 cup sorghum
- 1 teaspoon freshly ground black pepper

EGGS

- 4 teaspoons canola oil
- 6 large eggs
- Kosher salt and freshly ground black pepper
- 4 teaspoons unsalted butter

To make the bacon, preheat the oven to 325°F. In a large Dutch oven over medium-high heat, sear the bacon 1 portion at a time, about 2 minutes on each side. Remove the bacon and drain off all but 2 tablespoons of the fat from the pan. Add the onion and garlic and cook until light brown, about 3 minutes. Stir in the brown sugar and cook for another minute. Add the wine, beer, and cider and simmer until the liquid is reduced by half, about 6 minutes. Return the seared bacon to the Dutch oven and add the chicken stock. Bring to a simmer, and simmer for about 10 minutes. Add the oregano sprigs. Place in the oven and cook for 1½ hours. Remove from the oven; increase the oven temperature to 450°F.

Meanwhile, make the topping. Soak the raisins in the bourbon for 1 hour at room temperature. Drain the raisins and place in a medium bowl. Add the almonds, pecans, sunflower seeds, sorghum, and pepper and toss to mix well.

To make the fried eggs, heat the oil in a 10 to 12-inch skillet over low heat. Crack 2 eggs into a bowl and season with salt and pepper. Increase the heat under the skillet to medium-high and add the butter. When the butter is melted, add the eggs and cover the skillet with a lid. Cook the eggs for 20 to 30 seconds, until the egg whites are opaque. Transfer the eggs to a warm plate. Repeat with the remaining eggs, and keep warm.

To finish, remove the bacon from the braising broth. Strain and skim the fat from the broth. Keep the broth warm. Slice the bacon pieces into ¾-inch slices, place in a baking dish, and top with the nut-raisin topping. Place in the 450°F oven and bake for 5 minutes, or until the bacon is crisp on the edges and the topping is toasted. Place in 4 serving bowls and pour ½ cup of the braising broth into each bowl. Top each with a fried egg and serve.

TWO

From the Cupboard and Garden

The American table brings together a true feast: family, nature's bounty, and a place to share the two. During the busy year we plan and grow our gardens; in the summer months we stock our pantry shelves by harvesting fresh herbs and vegetables and preserving, jarring, and saving for another day. In this chapter, you will find those pantry treasures—the perfect accompaniments to accent and enhance everyday meals, holiday extravaganzas, and celebrations of every kind—and the dishes that show off the best of our garden.

The chapter starts with sauces, because in Kansas and Missouri, we believe that sauces can make a good meal great. Of course, barbecue sauce is the backbone of our condiment culture, so that leads the parade. But we can't depend on it for everything, so you'll also find hot sauce, steak sauce, and a killer dry rub that you'll use over and over again.

My wife will always make sure there's something sweet on the table, such as her Strawberry, Lemon, and Thyme Jam (page 32) or Cranberry-Quince Preserves (page 35), as her simple reminder to guests to put sugar on something.

We capture the great flavors of our garden in a variety of pickles and potato salads. Potato salad is one of the most common Midwestern side dishes, making an appearance at every barbecue, picnic, and family get-together. But I rarely eat it—it's usually overdressed, overcooked, and just plain sad. That's unfortunate, because if made correctly, potato salad is a great addition to any outdoor meal. In this chapter, I have included a few variations that I have created throughout the years. I left the mayonnaise at home. Remember, you can always mix and match the potatoes—just mind the cooking times!

At the end of a meal, if your child is anything like our son, Colin, then he or she has at least tried all the sauces, dips, and jams, and from that perspective you can call that meal a success! ★C.G.

BBQ SAUCE

★ MAKES 4½ CUPS ★

Barbecue sauce is a source of pride in Kansas City, where recipes are sometimes handed down through generations. I wasn't lucky enough to get one handed to me, so it's been a journey for us to make a great sauce. Some people like theirs sweet, some spicy, some with lots of vinegar, some with lots of pepper. I would say ours is a little bit more on the vinegary side, with a touch of sweetness. ★ C.G.

2½ cups ketchup

¾ cup firmly packed light brown sugar

1 tablespoon Simple Syrup (page 142)

2 tablespoons molasses

1 tablespoon apple cider vinegar

4 teaspoons Worcestershire sauce

1 tablespoon yellow mustard

1½ teaspoons liquid smoke

2½ teaspoons BBQ Dry Rub (page 30)

½ teaspoon freshly ground black pepper

½ teaspoon garlic powder

¾ teaspoon onion powder

1 teaspoon mustard powder

¼ teaspoon cayenne pepper

1 cup water

Combine all the ingredients in a medium saucepan and simmer for one hour.

Allow the sauce to cool to room temperature, then transfer to an airtight container. The sauce will keep in the refrigerator for up to 1 month.

BBQ
SAUCE
(OPPOSITE)

HOT SAUCE
(PAGE 28)

STEAK SAUCE
(PAGE 29)

HOT SAUCE

★ ★ ★ ★ ★ ★ ★ ★

MAKES 6 CUPS

One of my old *sous chefs* made this recipe years ago. You can use this on wings, fried chicken, eggs, steak—you name it. It has a ton of flavor and is fairly mild for a hot sauce. If it's not hot enough for you, add a couple of teaspoons of cayenne pepper. ★ C.G.

1 pound fresh Fresno chiles, stems removed

1 pound fresh Fresno chiles, charred (see Note)

2 bell peppers, charred (see Note), stems and seeds removed

2 cups apple cider vinegar

2 cups water

1 cup diced yellow onion

¼ cup honey

3 cloves garlic, smashed

2 tablespoons kosher salt

In a large sauce pan, combine the Fresno chiles, bell peppers, vinegar, water, onion, honey, garlic, and salt; simmer over medium heat for 25 minutes to bring all the flavors together.

Remove the pot from the heat and carefully transfer the hot liquid to a heavy-duty blender. Puree the mixture until smooth and then strain through a fine-mesh sieve. Allow the hot sauce to cool to room temperature, then transfer to an airtight container. The sauce will keep in the refrigerator for up to 1 month.

 Char the Fresno chiles and bell peppers over an open flame or under the broiler until the skin is blackened on all sides. Remove the stem and seeds from the bell peppers, but keep the Fresno peppers intact.

STEAK SAUCE

MAKES 8 CUPS

When I met my wife, she put A.1. Steak Sauce on every steak that graced her plate. It killed me a little bit inside every time I saw it. I set out to make my own steak sauce that she would like better. Ultimately, I lost out to the old English sauce—at least as far as Megan is concerned. Everyone else loves my version! The secret ingredient: oyster sauce. You can use ¼ cup chopped anchovies instead, if you prefer. ★ C.G.

2 tablespoons vegetable oil

1 medium yellow onion, diced

4 cloves garlic, chopped

2 cups red wine (any kind is fine)

4 cups home-preserved tomatoes or good-quality canned whole tomatoes, such as San Marzano, with juice

1 tablespoon tomato paste

1 cup oyster sauce

1 cup chopped dried plums (prunes)

Finely grated zest and juice of 2 oranges

Juice of 2 lemons

¼ cup Worcestershire sauce

¼ cup sherry vinegar

1 tablespoon BBQ Dry Rub (page 30) or your favorite kind

1 tablespoon Hot Sauce (page 28) or store-bought

1 tablespoon freshly ground black pepper

Heat the oil in a medium sauce pan over high heat. Cook the onions and garlic in the oil until translucent, about 3 minutes. Add the red wine and cook until reduced by two-thirds, about 10 minutes. Add the tomatoes and tomato paste and bring to a simmer. Add the oyster sauce, dried plums, orange zest, orange juice, lemon juice, Worcestershire sauce, vinegar, dry rub, hot sauce, and pepper; decrease the heat to low, and simmer for another 20 minutes.

Transfer the sauce from the pan to a heatproof, airtight container and refrigerate overnight. When thoroughly chilled, puree in a stand mixer. Store in an airtight container in the refrigerator for up to 1 month.

BBQ DRY RUB

★ MAKES 4 CUPS ★

Barbecue rub is as central to Midwestern cooking as cumin and chiles are in South America or as curry is in Southeast Asia: It defines our culture. If you're lucky enough, you have your very own. Mine has evolved over the years. It started as some brown sugar, salt, and chili seasoning and has progressed into something more complex. When I started cooking professionally, I started to understand what I needed to look for (or taste for!) when making a good seasoning. When you're trained as a professional chef you're taught very specific disciplines, and in western European cooking you rely on salt and pepper as the only dry ingredients to put on proteins unless you're curing something. That's when it hit me. Some of the same qualities and flavors that you use in quick-curing something like salmon translate well to rubbing meat for smoking. The base of my rub came from the base of my salmon cure. It's salty, sweet, and herbaceous. Just tweak the flavoring as you like, and it's perfect. ★ C.G.

1¾ cups kosher salt

1 cup firmly packed light brown sugar

1 cup granulated sugar

¼ cup onion powder

¼ cup garlic powder

2 tablespoons smoked paprika

1 tablespoon crushed red pepper flakes

1 tablespoon ground mustard

1½ teaspoons chili powder

1 teaspoon freshly ground white pepper

1 teaspoon freshly ground black pepper

In a large bowl, combine the salt, both sugars, onion powder, garlic powder, paprika, red pepper flakes, ground mustard, chili powder, white pepper, and black pepper. Transfer the rub to an airtight container and store at room temperature for up to 1 month.

APPLE-BOURBON BUTTER

Makes 2 cups

For me, the first taste of autumn is always a spoonful of fresh apple butter slathered on a warm slice of bread. Apple butter is an amazingly versatile condiment—it can be spread on sweet morning pastries, used to coat the bottom of a winter pie, or served with savory meats like pork or pheasant. This adult version features the rich caramel flavor of bourbon, but you can substitute apple cider for the bourbon and water in this recipe, if you prefer. While most apple butter recipes require overnight cooking in a slow cooker, this recipe comes together in just a few hours. ★ M.G.

6 apples (preferably Braeburn, Honeycrisp, or McIntosh), peeled, cored, and cut into cubes

2 cups water

1 cup plus 2 tablespoons bourbon

1½ cups firmly packed light brown sugar

1 teaspoon ground cinnamon

½ teaspoon ground nutmeg

½ teaspoon ground cloves

Juice of 1 lemon, strained

In a large heavy sauce pan, combine the apples, water, and 1 cup of the bourbon. Cook over medium heat until the apples are tender, about 15 minutes. Remove from the heat and add the brown sugar, cinnamon, nutmeg, cloves, and lemon juice. Using a handheld immersion blender, purée the mixture until smooth.

Cook the apple mixture over medium heat, stirring occasionally, until the mixture bubbles slowly and thickens to a paste, about 1½ hours. Remove the pot from the heat and stir in the remaining 2 tablespoons bourbon. Let the apple butter cool to room temperature, then transfer to an airtight container and refrigerate. The apple butter will keep in the refrigerator for up to 2 weeks.

Alternatively, this apple butter may be jarred for longer storage or gift-giving. Use sterile glass jam jars (two 1-cup jars or one 2-cup jar) and follow the manufacturer's instructions for proper preserving.

STRAWBERRY, LEMON, and THYME JAM

MAKES 3 CUPS

2 pounds strawberries, hulled and quartered

2 cups sugar

Finely grated zest and juice of 1 lemon

1 bunch thyme

Strawberries are the sign of spring in the West and a turn toward summer in the Midwest. When strawberries are good, you need to do nothing more than eat them right off the stem. This recipe allows the best berries to be transformed into a jam that brings summer to the table any time of the year. Here I try to re-create my grandmother Frances's sweet strawberry jam, one she made by memory and never wrote down. I add my favorite herb, thyme, which I often use in sweet things for a little taste of earth. This recipe is delicious paired with Corn Fritters with Fresh Sheep's Milk Cheese (page 21) or folded into whipped butter for breakfast. ★ M.G.

In a large saucepan, combine the strawberries, sugar, lemon zest, lemon juice, and thyme sprigs. Cook the mixture over medium-high heat until the mixture bubbles and the berries begin to break down, 8 to 10 minutes. Decrease the heat to medium-low and simmer until the color begins to deepen and the fruit begins to have a shiny appearance, 25 to 30 minutes.

Dip a spoon into the hot, bubbly jam; the jam should coat the spoon. Let the spoon sit at room temperature for 2 to 3 minutes, then run your finger across the back of the spoon; if the jam runs slowly and beads up along the edges, it is done, but if the jam is loose and watery, continue to cook until it reaches a firmer texture. Once the jam has cooked long enough, use a fork to remove as many of the thyme springs as possible; a little left in the jam itself is OK. Let the jam cool to room temperature, then transfer to an airtight container or containers and refrigerate. The jam will keep in the refrigerator for up to 2 weeks.

Alternatively, this jam may be jarred for longer storage or gift-giving. Use sterile glass jam jars (three 1-cup jars or one 3-cup jar) and follow the manufacturer's instructions for proper preserving.

SPICY TOMATO JAM

★ MAKES 2 CUPS ★

This jam is spicy and sweet and a good way to use overripened tomatoes. It makes a great accompaniment to cheese or any grilled meat. You can also use it to make a killer BLT with cooked regular bacon and the braised bacon (see page 22)—alongside sliced fresh tomatoes, this jam gives the sandwich a rich taste of summer. ★ M.G.

2 tablespoons extra-virgin olive oil

1 medium shallot, minced

3 cloves garlic, minced

1 tablespoon minced fresh ginger

1½ pounds tomatoes, seeded and chopped

1 cup sugar

½ cup red wine vinegar

1 teaspoon crushed red pepper flakes

1 teaspoon smoked paprika

Heat the oil in a medium sauce pan over medium heat. Add the shallot, garlic, and ginger and cook until they become translucent, 3 to 4 minutes. Add the tomatoes, bring to a simmer, and simmer for 2 minutes to bring the flavors together. Add the sugar, vinegar, red pepper flakes, and paprika. Continue to simmer on low heat until reduced and thick, about 1 hour and 10 minutes. Let cool, then transfer to an airtight container. The jam will keep in the refrigerator for 2 weeks.

Alternatively, this jam may be jarred for longer storage or gift-giving. Use sterile glass jam jars (three 1-cup jars or one 3-cup jar) and follow the manufacturer's instructions for proper preserving.

Cranberry-Quince
Preserves

★ **M A K E S   4   C U P S** ★

There is nothing like the scent of quince in the kitchen: that bright, floral fragrance in the middle of winter. This fruit is something of a chameleon, with a bright yellow skin and a tough white flesh that, once cooked, becomes a gorgeous, sweet, pink treat. Cranberries make a good addition to the quince, adding a brighter pop of red and some tartness to the preserves. Quince and cranberry are a classic winter combination, and both work with a variety of other flavors, so you can make this recipe your own by adding brandy, clove, cardamom, or ginger, to name just a few possibilities. Here we keep it simple with citrus, vanilla, and star anise. ★ M.G.

6 quinces, peeled, cored, and finely diced

3 cups water

2 cups sugar

1 cup freshly squeezed orange juice

Peel of 1 orange

3 whole star anise

1 vanilla bean, split and scraped

2 cups cranberries

Juice of 1 lemon

In a large sauce pan, combine the quinces, sugar, water, ½ cup of the orange juice, orange peel, star anise, and vanilla bean pod and seeds. Heat over medium heat and simmer, stirring occasionally, until the quince pieces soften and the liquid reduces to a thick syrup, about 1 hour.

Remove the pot from the heat and, using a potato masher, press the quince to mash slightly. Stir in the remaining ½ cup orange juice and the cranberries. Cook over medium heat until the cranberries pop and break down, about 20 minutes.

Remove the pot from the heat and stir in the lemon juice. Remove the vanilla bean pod and whole star anise. Let the preserves cool to room temperature, then transfer to an airtight container and refrigerate. The preserves will keep in the refrigerator for up to 2 weeks.

Alternatively, the preserves may be jarred for longer storage or gift-giving. Use sterile glass jam jars (four 1-cup jars or two 1-pint jars) and follow the manufacturer's instructions for proper preserving.

HONEYED GOAT CHEESE SPREAD

MAKES 6 CUPS

Combining whipped goat cheese and honey creates a sweet-salty spread that's perfect as a predinner snack or on the brunch table with a pastry—or as a smear on crunchy toast any time of day. This recipe can also be made with other types of soft cheeses, such as fresh sheep's milk cheese, ricotta, or mild blue cheese. ★ M.G.

1 cup extra-virgin olive oil
12 cloves garlic, peeled
2 sprigs thyme
3 cups goat cheese, softened
1 cup cream cheese, softened
½ cup heavy cream
1 tablespoon honey
Kosher salt and freshly ground black pepper
Toasted sourdough or crusty French bread, for serving

In a small sauce pan, combine the oil, garlic, and thyme. Cook slowly over low heat, being careful not to brown or fry the garlic, until the garlic becomes very soft, about 20 minutes. Drain the oil from the garlic, reserving the oil and placing the garlic in the bowl of a stand mixer; discard the thyme. Using the stand mixer fitted with the paddle attachment, whip the garlic until it starts to mash. Add the goat cheese and cream cheese and whip for about 15 minutes to reach a perfectly smooth texture. Slowly add the heavy cream, and then add 2 tablespoons of the garlic oil (reserve the remaining garlic oil for another use) and whip for another 2 minutes to incorporate.

To serve, fill a glass jar or serving bowl with the whipped cheese and drizzle the honey over the top. Season with salt and pepper to taste. Serve the toasted bread on the side at room temperature. Any leftover whipped cheese may be stored in an airtight container in the refrigerator for up to 1 week.

QUICK PICKLES

Makes 4 cups

If you were to meet my father, chances are good you'd end up taking home a jar of his pickles. This recipe is an ode to my dad, the master of pickling. Green beans or peppers are his veggies of choice, but I use cucumbers, because hot Kansas summers produce the best cucumbers. In July and August, our family farm becomes a maze of colorful vegetables. Planting and pulling these gems of summer are among my favorite moments spent on the land with my dad. Our editor loves these bright, crunchy, vinegary pickles and wouldn't allow us to leave them out of this book! They add bright flavor to barbecue or fried chicken. For the best crunch, make the pickles fresh before serving. ★ C.G.

2 cups water
2 cucumbers, thinly sliced
1 tablespoon sugar
1 teaspoon kosher salt
½ medium yellow onion, thinly sliced
1½ teaspoons rice wine vinegar
Pinch of BBQ Dry Rub (page 30)

In a medium sauce pan, bring the water to a boil. In a medium bowl, toss the cucumbers with ½ tablespoon of the sugar and ½ teaspoon of the salt and set aside for 5 minutes. In a large bowl, toss the onions with the remaining ½ tablespoon sugar and the remaining ½ teaspoon salt and let sit for 5 minutes.

Thoroughly rinse the cucumbers under cold water, drain, and place in a large bowl. Pour the boiling water over the onions and stir to cook slightly. Once the onions have softened, after about 3 minutes, rinse the onions under cold water to stop the cooking process. Drain, and add the onions to the bowl with the cucumbers. Add the rice wine vinegar and toss with the vegetables.

To serve, fill a serving bowl or medium jar with the pickles and sprinkle the barbecue rub over the top. Leftover pickles may be stored in an airtight container in the refrigerator for up to 2 days; after that the cucumbers will become too soft.

Pickled Rhubarb
with Celery, Strawberries, and Black Pepper

★ MAKES 4 CUPS ★

Rhubarb grows everywhere, and we always have plenty in the spring and summer at my dad's house, at our house, at my sister's house, and at the farm. My dad loves it in rhubarb pie; that was his mother's specialty when he was growing up. But I love to pickle it with celery and wild green strawberries. For simplicity's sake, we used regular strawberries for this recipe, but if you stumble upon some green ones, grab 'em! ★ C.G.

2 cups water

1 cup apple cider vinegar

⅔ cup white wine vinegar

6 tablespoons sugar

4 teaspoons kosher salt

1 teaspoon freshly ground black pepper

1 pound rhubarb, peeled and sliced into ½-inch pieces

8 ounces celery, sliced ⅛ inch thick

8 ounces strawberries, thinly sliced

Mix the water, cider vinegar, white wine vinegar, sugar, salt, and pepper in a medium sauce pan and bring to a simmer over medium heat. In a large bowl, toss the rhubarb, celery, and strawberries. Pour the simmering liquid over the vegetables and mix well. Let cool to room temperature and then refrigerate, uncovered, overnight to let the flavors meld before serving. The vegetables will keep refrigerated in an airtight container for up to 3 days.

PICKLED GREEN TOMATOES

★ MAKES 6 CUPS ★

Between the heat and the drought in the dog days of a Midwest summer, tomato vines struggle to produce in their final weeks. Then, inevitably, we'll get a few rainstorms that produce a plethora of green tomatoes. We fry as many as we can eat, but there are always more left over, so we pickle the remaining haul. They've become one of my favorite summer treats. ★ C.G.

3 pounds small green tomatoes, quartered

1 medium red onion, sliced ⅛ inch thick

4 sprigs oregano

3 tablespoons kosher salt

1 tablespoon freshly cracked black pepper

4 cups red wine vinegar

1 cup water

1 cup white wine

12 cloves garlic, thinly sliced

¼ cup sugar

Place the tomatoes, onions, oregano, salt, and pepper in a large bowl and toss well. In a medium sauce pan over medium heat, bring the vinegar, water, white wine, garlic, and sugar to a simmer. Pour the simmering liquid over the vegetables and mix well. Let cool to room temperature and then refrigerate, uncovered, overnight to let the flavors meld before serving. The tomatoes will keep refrigerated in an airtight container for up to 3 days.

PICKLED GREEN TOMATOES
(PAGE 39)

PICKLED RHUBARB WITH
CELERY, STRAWBERRIES, AND
BLACK PEPPER (PAGE 38)

PICKLED RADISHES
(OPPOSITE)

Pickled Radishes

Along with tomatoes and rhubarb, we always have plenty of radishes during the summer months. I like to pickle them with mustard seeds and garlic. Pickled radishes are delicious added to crunchy summer greens in a salad, layered in a smoked turkey sandwich, or served as a snack alongside summer cocktails on the patio. ★ C.G.

10 large radishes, quartered (with greens still attached, if possible)

20 cloves garlic, peeled

2 teaspoons crushed red pepper flakes

1 teaspoon whole black peppercorns

2 cups apple cider vinegar

1 tablespoon mustard seeds

1 teaspoon kosher salt

1 teaspoon sugar

Place the radishes, garlic, red pepper flakes, and black peppercorns in a medium bowl. In a medium sauce pan, bring the vinegar, mustard seeds, salt, and sugar to a simmer over medium heat. Pour the simmering liquid over the vegetables and mix well. Let cool to room temperature and then refrigerate, uncovered, overnight to let the flavors meld before serving. The radishes will keep refrigerated in an airtight container for up to 3 days.

Pimm's Punch

PUNCH

1½ cups Pimm's No. 1

4 ounces rye whiskey, such as Old Overholt

¼ cup Caramel Simple Syrup (recipe follows)

¾ cup hulled and quartered strawberries

Finely grated zest and juice of 2 lemons

SERVING

Ginger ale (2½ ounces per serving)

Ice cubes

Lemon slices, for garnish

Cucumber slices (unpeeled), for garnish

Fresh sprigs mint, for garnish

To make the punch, whisk together the Pimm's, whiskey, caramel syrup, strawberries, lemon zest, and lemon juice in a large bowl. Cover the bowl and let the punch marinate in the refrigerator overnight, or preferably for 3 days.

Using a fine-mesh sieve, strain the Pimm's mixture into a pitcher, discarding the strawberries and lemon zest.

To serve, pour 2½ ounces ginger ale and 1½ ounces Pimm's mixture into a Collins glass. Top with ice cubes and garnish with a slice of lemon, a slice of cucumber, and a sprig of mint. The Pimm's mixture will keep in an airtight container in the refrigerator for up to 1 week.

Caramel Simple Syrup   Makes 2 cups

2 cups turbinado sugar (raw sugar)

1 cup boiling water

In a heavy sauce pan, heat the sugar (dry) over medium heat, carefully swirling the pan to dissolve the sugar evenly. Allow the sugar to cook to a medium amber color, 8 to 10 minutes.

Slowly whisk the boiling water into the hot sugar, being very careful that the hot caramel doesn't spatter. Thoroughly whisk the water and sugar together and bring to a rapid boil. Remove from the heat and let cool to room temperature. Transfer the cooled syrup to an airtight container and keep chilled until ready to use, up to 1 month. The simple syrup can also be used in iced tea and in other cocktails.

This potato salad is a tribute to the classic Irish combination of corned beef and hash and is full of kick. Find a good-quality corned beef that's been cooked long enough that it falls apart nicely. If you don't have pickled okra in the pantry like we always do, feel free to use any store-bought variety. The salt, vinegar, and the brine of the corned beef definitely call for a cold beer alongside this salad. ★ C.G.

- 2 pounds fingerling potatoes
- 1 tablespoon kosher salt, plus more for seasoning
- 2 tablespoons vegetable oil
- 1 shallot, minced
- 2 cloves garlic, minced
- 1 cup home-preserved tomatoes or good-quality canned chopped tomatoes, such as San Marzano, with juice
- 1 tablespoon red wine vinegar
- 1 tablespoon Hot Sauce (page 28) or store-bought
- 1/3 cup olive oil
- 1/2 cup shredded corned beef
- 1/3 cup sliced pickled okra
- 1/3 cup diced red onion
- 1/3 cup diced celery
- 1 bunch flat-leaf parsley, stemmed and chopped
- Freshly ground black pepper
- 1/2 cup chopped scallions, for garnish

FINGERLING POTATO SALAD WITH SPICY TOMATO, CORNED BEEF, AND PICKLED OKRA

Place the potatoes in a large pot and add water to cover by 1 inch. Add the 1 tablespoon salt and bring to a boil. Cook for about 5 minutes, until the potatoes are just fork-tender. Drain the potatoes and let them cool to room temperature. When cool, slice into 1/2-inch slices.

Heat the vegetable oil in a small sauce pan over medium heat. Add the shallots and garlic and cook for 2 minutes, stirring frequently; do not let them brown. Add the tomatoes and continue to cook for 4 minutes, until the tomatoes begin to break down. If using whole tomatoes, use an immersion blender to chop them a bit, but do not puree; large pieces are desired. Add the vinegar and hot sauce, decrease the heat to medium-low, and cook until all the liquid is cooked out and only tomato remains, about 6 minutes. Add the olive oil to the tomato sauce and set the sauce aside.

To finish, place the potatoes in a large bowl. Gently fold in the tomato sauce. Add the corned beef and okra, red onion, celery, and parsley, and gently fold again. Season to taste with salt and pepper. Garnish with the chopped scallions.

YUKON GOLD POTATO SALAD WITH SUMMER CORN, COUNTRY HAM, AND GARLICKY LEMON-CHIVE DRESSING (OPPOSITE)

BABY RED POTATOES WITH BLUE CHEESE, COUNTRY HAM, WHITE BEANS, AND GLAZED PEARL ONIONS (PAGE 47)

CUCUMBER-DILL SALAD (PAGE 46)

SERVES 4 TO 6

This is a great summer salad that features sweet corn, a bright and tangy dressing, and all those country ham ends you've been collecting. We reserve this salad for special family dinners or summer gatherings like Labor Day picnics and Father's Day. The kids and I try to give Colby a day off from cooking, and this is the perfect recipe for the three of us to create together—the little ones can help shuck the corn, juice the lemons, and smash the garlic. Of course, eventually Colby takes over because he can't help himself! ★ M.G.

- **2 pounds Yukon gold potatoes**
- **1 tablespoon kosher salt, plus more for seasoning**
- **1 teaspoon unsalted butter**
- **¾ cup fresh corn kernels (from about 1 ear of corn)**
- **1¼ cups extra-virgin olive oil**
- **2 tablespoons finely grated lemon zest**
- **Juice of 2 lemons**
- **1 bunch flat-leaf parsley, stemmed and chopped**
- **5 cloves garlic, smashed or pressed through a garlic press**
- **½ teaspoon crushed red pepper flakes**
- **Freshly ground black pepper**
- **⅓ cup small-dice country ham**

YUKON GOLD POTATO SALAD WITH SUMMER CORN, COUNTRY HAM, AND GARLICKY LEMON-CHIVE DRESSING

Place the potatoes in a large pot and add water to cover by 1 inch. Add the 1 tablespoon salt and bring to a boil. Cook until potatoes are just fork-tender, about 8 minutes. Drain the potatoes and let them cool to room temperature. Quarter the potatoes and place in a large bowl.

In a small sauté pan, melt the butter over medium-high heat. Add the corn to the butter and cook until the corn is lightly browned, about 2 minutes.

Place the olive oil, lemon zest and juice, parsley, garlic, and red pepper flakes in a medium bowl. Mix well and season the dressing with salt and pepper.

Add the corn and ham to the potatoes. Add the dressing and mix well. Adjust the seasoning and serve.

CUCUMBER-DILL SALAD

Serves 4 to 6

This is the classic cucumber and dill salad. I love the brightness of these vegetables and flavors, so rather than muddying them up with mayonnaise and mustard, we use vinegar and olive oil. When this salad is really cold, it's cleansing and satisfying. ★ C.G.

4 medium cucumbers, sliced or julienned

½ medium red onion, sliced into very thin rings

2 tablespoons kosher salt

¼ cup red wine vinegar

2 tablespoons extra-virgin olive oil

½ teaspoon smoked paprika

2 ounces dry firm goat cheese

½ teaspoon crushed red pepper flakes

¼ cup loosely packed sprigs dill

Place the cucumbers and red onion in a large bowl or baking dish. Sprinkle with the salt and toss to coat evenly. Let sit at room temperature for 2 hours. Drain the vegetables and squeeze out the remaining liquid.

In a small bowl, combine the vinegar, olive oil, and paprika; mix well. In a large bowl, toss the cucumbers and onions with the dressing. Crumble and sprinkle the goat cheese over the top, then the red pepper flakes, and finally the dill sprigs.

BABY RED POTATOES WITH BLUE CHEESE, COUNTRY HAM, WHITE BEANS, AND GLAZED PEARL ONIONS

SERVES 4 TO 6

★ ★ ★ ★ ★ ★ ★ ★

This is a fun red, white, and blue salad that would be great around the Fourth of July. Find yourself a good blue cheese such as Maytag that you have to crumble yourself and that has a good tang to it. Stay away from packaged crumbles! You can use canned white beans, or use your favorite recipe for cooked white beans. ★ C.G.

2 pounds small red potatoes

1 tablespoon plus 1 teaspoon kosher salt, plus more for seasoning

12 pearl onions, quartered

1½ cups chicken stock

1 teaspoon sugar

1 cup extra-virgin olive oil

¼ cup sherry vinegar

Juice of 1 lemon

1 bunch flat-leaf parsley, stemmed and chopped

1 medium shallot, minced

2 tablespoons drained capers, chopped

1 tablespoon chopped fresh chives

1 cup canned white beans, such as navy beans

2 celery ribs, thinly sliced on the diagonal

1 small red onion, diced

¼ cup small-dice country ham

Freshly ground black pepper

¾ cup crumbled blue cheese

Place the potatoes in a large pot and add water to cover by 1 inch. Add the 1 tablespoon salt and bring to a boil. Cook for about 5 minutes, or until the potatoes are just fork-tender. Drain the potatoes and let them cool to room temperature. Quarter the potatoes and place in a large bowl.

Place the pearl onions in a 2-quart sauce pan with the stock, the 1 teaspoon salt, and the sugar. Simmer over medium heat until the onions are cooked through and the liquid has evaporated, about 20 minutes.

Place the olive oil, sherry vinegar, lemon juice, parsley, shallot, capers, and chives in a medium bowl and mix well.

Add the pearl onions, beans, celery, red onion, and ham to the potatoes and gently fold together. Add the dressing and gently fold again to combine. Season the salad to taste with salt and pepper. Top with the crumbled blue cheese.

THREE

Cast Iron
and Dutch Ovens

I pretty much divide the year into two parts: when I can cook outside, and when I head back indoors and cook everything in Dutch ovens and cast-iron pans. Since we live in the Midwest, where winters are long, we have four or five Dutch ovens and just as many cast-iron pans, which get a lot of use during the colder months. The braises and stews that come from these pots—like Madeira-Braised Chicken with Sour Cherries (page 51) and Cider-Braised Brisket (page 60)—are both rich and satisfying.

Dutch ovens are a lot of fun to master because you can use them on the stovetop, in the oven, or even outdoors. When I went on Cub Scouts camping trips growing up, my mom or dad would pack a ready-to-cook meal in one of these handy ovens. Once camp was set up, it was placed next to the campfire to create a delicious roasted dinner. Whether you use your Dutch oven on the stovetop (where it will act like its own self-contained oven) or inside the oven, be sure to keep a tight lid on it to seal in the steam and juices for a slow, even cooking process. A few rules: Use hearty root vegetables and tougher cuts of meat that can withstand long cooking times; make sure there is enough braising liquid in the pot so that it doesn't dry out or burn; and add layers of flavors with celery, chopped onion, herbs, and seasonings. The result will be a perfect Dutch-oven dinner.

Cast-iron pans are such reliable workhorses in the kitchen that they're often handed down from generation to generation—as mine were. They're heavy and thick, they can stand up to abuse over the years, and they hold heat consistently, which makes them perfect for browning meats and stovetop frying, as in Sorghum-Glazed Pheasant (page 57) and Panfried BBQ Pork Chops with Tomato-Horseradish Sauce (page 54). And when cast-iron pans are seasoned properly, they're practically nonstick.

Seasoning a cast-iron pan means layering and baking on coats of oil—the oil seeps into the pores of the pan, creating a flavor barrier for many dishes to come. Begin by washing and drying the pan (use little or no soap), then rub 1 to 2 tablespoons of your preferred oil into the pan with a paper towel until the cast iron has a matte sheen. Vegetable oil is most commonly used, but flaxseed oil is also a good choice. Then put the pan in a preheated 350°F oven for an hour or so. To clean the seasoned pan after cooking, just wipe it out, using water if necessary. Make sure to dry it promptly and to wipe with more oil as needed to keep it seasoned. ★ C.G.

CHICKEN
and
DUMPLINGS

★ ★ ★ ★ ★ ★ ★ ★

SERVES 4 TO 6

Chicken and dumplings was my sister Amy's favorite dinner. This was a legendary dish around our house, which we were informed was reserved for very, very special events. Strangely, it was only served on my sister's birthday. I remember it being warm and comfortable. And it tasted extra special because it was always there on Amy's day.... ★ C.G.

STEW

- 1 (3½- to 4-pound) chicken, legs and thighs removed and separated
- 6 cups chicken stock
- 6 ounces slab bacon, cubed
- 2 tablespoons canola oil
- 4 carrots, peeled and sliced ¼ inch thick
- 4 celery ribs, sliced ¼ inch thick
- 1 medium yellow onion, chopped
- 2 fresh bay leaves
- 4 cloves garlic, thinly sliced
- 6 tablespoons unbleached all-purpose flour
- ¾ cup Sherry
- ¼ cup milk

DUMPLINGS

- 2 cups unbleached all-purpose flour
- 1 tablespoon baking powder
- 1 cup buttermilk (full-fat if you can get it)
- 3 tablespoons unsalted butter
- Salt and freshly ground black pepper
- ½ teaspoon minced fresh flat-leaf parsley
- ½ teaspoon minced fresh oregano

To make the stew, place the chicken body (without the legs and thighs) in a large Dutch oven and cover with the stock. Bring to a simmer, then decrease the heat to medium-low and cook for 10 to 12 minutes, until the internal temperature near but not touching the bone is 160°F. Remove the chicken from the broth and chill for 1 hour. Cook the stock for another 8 to 10 minutes, until reduced to about 4½ cups.

Remove the skin from the chicken carcass and cut the meat from the bones. Slice the chicken breast and reserve on a plate. In a large Dutch oven over medium-high heat, brown the bacon for about 5 minutes, then transfer to a plate. Add the chicken legs and thighs to the Dutch oven and cook for about 8 minutes on each side. Remove from the pot and reserve on the plate with the chicken breast.

Add the oil and raise the heat to medium-high. Add the carrots, celery, onion, and bay leaves. Cook for about 5 minutes. Add the garlic and cook for another 2 minutes. Stir in the flour. Add the Sherry and scrape up the brown bits on the bottom of the pot. Stir in the reduced stock and milk. Bring to a simmer, then decrease the heat to medium-low, add the bacon and the chicken breast, legs and thighs, and cook until the chicken is fully cooked, about 1 hour.

Meanwhile, to make the dumplings, butter a casserole dish. In a medium bowl, mix the flour and baking powder. In a small sauce pan, warm the buttermilk and butter until just warm to the touch and the butter is fully melted. Stir the buttermilk mixture into the flour mixture. Season with salt and pepper and mix with a wooden spoon until smooth. Fold in the parsley and oregano. Using 2 large spoons, divide the dumpling dough into 8 golf ball–size balls and place in the buttered casserole dish. If you would like nice uniformly round dumplings, you can rub the palm of your hands with a little softened butter and form the dumplings into smoother balls.

Bring the stew back to a simmer, if necessary, and arrange the dumplings on the top of the stew, leaving a bit of room between each one. Simmer for about 30 minutes, or until the dumplings are cooked through with no doughy texture. Serve immediately.

MADEIRA-BRAISED CHICKEN WITH SOUR CHERRIES

★ **SERVES 4** ★

Braised sour cherries have such a rich, deep flavor that they pair nicely with chicken or game in a dark broth. Here the broth and the chicken get an extra layer of richness from Madeira, a fortified wine (dry Sherry can also be used). Serve this with Slow-Cooked Pale Ale Barley (recipe follows) and a light-bodied red wine, such as Pinot Noir. ★ C.G.

1 (3½-pound) chicken, cut into 10 pieces

Kosher salt and freshly ground black pepper

2 tablespoons vegetable oil

2 medium shallots, chopped

4 cloves garlic, chopped

4 cups pitted fresh sour cherries, thawed frozen sour cherries, or fresh Bing cherries (see Note, page 53)

2 cups Madeira or dry Sherry

2 tablespoons fresh thyme leaves

1 fresh bay leaf (see Note, page 53)

2 cups chicken stock

2 tablespoons sherry vinegar

Slow Cooked Pale Ale Barley (recipe follows), for serving

Preheat the oven to 325°F. Season the chicken pieces all over with salt and pepper. Heat the oil in a large Dutch oven over medium-high heat. Working in batches if needed, add the chicken pieces to the Dutch oven and brown well, about 4 minutes per side. Decrease the heat to medium and add the shallots, garlic, and 2 cups of the cherries. Cook until the shallots and garlic are soft and translucent, about 3 minutes. Add the Madeira, thyme, and bay leaf. Cook until the liquid is reduced by half, about 10 minutes. Add the stock and vinegar and bring to a simmer. Put the lid on the Dutch oven and place in the oven. Braise for 2 hours, or until the meat pulls easily from the bone.

Remove from the oven, add the remaining 2 cups cherries, and serve with the barley (recipe follows).

Continued

Slow-Cooked Pale Ale Barley   Serves 6

Pearl barley is *so* good when it's cooked with some rich stock and a little butter. Making this dish is like preparing risotto: It requires frequent stirring as you add the liquid in increments and keeping careful watch to see that the barley cooks evenly and doesn't stick to the bottom of the pan. But the results are worth the effort. This is a great side dish to serve with grilled or braised meat, and it's a delicious alternative to the standard potatoes or rice. ★ C.G.

2 cups chicken stock

2 cups pale ale

3 tablespoons unsalted butter

1 small yellow onion, chopped

2 cloves garlic, minced

1½ cups pearl barley

1 dried bay leaf

¼ cup toasted chopped pecans

In a small sauce pan, heat the stock and pale ale over medium heat.

In a medium sauce pan, melt 2 tablespoons of the butter over medium heat until it bubbles. Add the onion and garlic and sauté for 2 minutes, or until soft and translucent. Add the barley and continue to cook for another 2 minutes, lightly toasting the barley. Add the bay leaf and 2 cups of the warmed stock mixture; bring the mixture to a boil. Decrease the heat to medium-low and simmer until most of the stock is absorbed, stirring frequently, about 5 minutes.

Add the remaining hot stock ½ cup at a time, stirring frequently and allowing each addition of the stock to be absorbed before adding more, until the barley is tender, about 50 minutes.

Remove the bay leaf. Fold in the remaining 1 tablespoon butter and the toasted pecans, and serve.

NOTE Fresh sour cherries have a short season in the summer. Look for them in grocery stores or at farmers' markets. Frozen sour cherries, thawed, or fresh Bing cherries can be used in a pinch, but don't use dried cherries. A fresh bay leaf is preferred in this dish, but you can use dried if necessary. Fresh bay leaves are available at some specialty stores and online at **Penzeys Spices (www.penzeys.com).**

PANFRIED BBQ PORK CHOPS *with* TOMATO-HORSERADISH SAUCE

SERVES 4

Pork chops are the go-to dish in the Midwest for an easy, inexpensive, and satisfying meal. My mom often cooked pork chops with apples and sauerkraut in the fall and with preserved tomatoes and rice in the late winter. School nights and hectic evenings slowed down around the table, where my family recounted the day's activities. My dad checked on homework assignments, and my twerpy older brother took a break from annoying me so we could all enjoy mom's cooking. Now my mom's pork chop recipe, updated through Colby's Kansas barbecue roots and paired with Dutch Oven–Roasted Carrots with Brown Sugar and Carrot Top Crumble (page 59), creates new memories for our kids at the dinner table. Note that the sauce needs to be refrigerated overnight in order to bring all the flavors together. ★ M.G.

For the sauce, place the tomatoes, vinegar, horseradish, honey, garlic, and bay leaves in a small sauce pan. Bring to a simmer over medium-high heat and cook until reduced by half, about 20 minutes. Let cool, uncovered, then refrigerate overnight. Bring to room temperature before continuing with the rest of the recipe.

For the pork chops, generously rub the chops with the dry rub. Heat the oil in a large cast-iron pan over medium-high heat. Add the seasoned pork chops and brown on each side, about 4 minutes total. Add the butter, shallots, garlic, and thyme. Cook, basting the pork chops frequently with the warmed tomato sauce, until the internal temperature hits 140°F on an instant-read thermometer, 2 to 3 minutes longer. Serve with the extra sauce alongside.

TOMATO-HORSERADISH SAUCE

2 (14-ounce) jars home-preserved tomatoes or good-quality canned chopped tomatoes

1 cup sherry vinegar

¼ cup prepared white horseradish

¼ cup honey

4 cloves garlic, smashed and chopped

2 fresh bay leaves (see Note, page 53)

PORK CHOPS

4 (6-ounce) pork loin chops

¼ cup BBQ Dry Rub (page 30)

¼ cup vegetable oil

4 tablespoons (½ stick) unsalted butter, softened

4 small shallots, sliced

8 cloves garlic, peeled

2 bunches thyme

Wild game is notoriously difficult to cook properly. Not to mention that too many hunters recklessly skin game birds and only keep the breast, which is the easiest part to overcook, giving game birds a reputation for being dry. Pheasant has a rich flavor, like duck, yet is as lean as chicken. But unlike chicken, you can slightly undercook the breast to make it juicier. Here we pair the bird with a sauce that combines the sweet, nutty flavor of sorghum with a hoppy beer that adds a slightly bitter component; together, they perfectly complement the game bird. We use farm-raised pheasant in order to get more consistent results; you can ask your local butcher to order and split one for you. But if you do choose to shoot a wild pheasant, be sure to pluck the bird the old-fashioned way. ★ C.G.

1 cup sorghum

1/3 cup bitter, hoppy beer, such as IPA

2 tablespoons vegetable oil

1 (2- to 3-pound) pheasant, split

2 medium yellow onions, sliced 1/4 inch thick

5 sprigs fresh thyme

5 sprigs fresh oregano

1 dried bay leaf

Slow Cooker Grits (recipe follows), for serving

SORGHUM-GLAZED PHEASANT

In a small bowl, whisk the sorghum and the beer until well blended. Set aside.

Heat the vegetable oil in a large cast-iron pan over medium-high heat until the oil just begins to smoke. Decrease the heat to medium. Add the pheasant halves, skin side down, and brown for 5 minutes, or until golden. Flip the pieces over and cook for another 2 minutes. Remove the pheasant and put on a plate. Remove the pan from the heat and let rest for 2 minutes to cool slightly.

Add the onions, thyme sprigs, oregano sprigs, and bay leaf to the pan. Lay the pheasant halves, skin side up, on the onions and herbs and brush with the sorghum mixture. Cook over medium heat for 5 to 8 minutes, brushing with the sorghum glaze every few minutes, until the internal temperature of the leg reaches 155°F on an instant-read thermometer. Brush one more time before you serve. If you want the birds a little less done, bring the temperature of the leg to 148° to 150°F. Remove the bay leaf before serving with the grits (recipe follows).

Continued

Slow Cooker Grits   Makes 6 cups

People tell me all the time that they don't like grits. I know why. Their moms or grandmas probably used instant grits, cooked them in water, put a pat of butter on top, and sprinkled them with iodized salt. I don't like them like that, either. We use butter, cream, good cheese, and a little love. The other issue with grits is that they burn easily in a regular pot if you don't watch them closely. We use the double-boiler system at the restaurants, with a mixing bowl and a pot of boiling water. But that's too complicated at home, so I use a slow cooker. It's easy; you just have to keep a good stir on them. You can serve these grits for dinner with shrimp, chicken, or barbecue. Or make them the night before and reheat them in the morning over medium heat, using a little milk or cream to loosen them up. Then serve for breakfast with eggs and bacon. ★ C.G.

2 cups coarse-ground white grits

2 cups heavy cream

2 cups milk

3 tablespoons unsalted butter

1 cup grated good-quality aged cheddar cheese

Kosher salt and freshly ground black pepper

In a 6-quart slow cooker, combine the grits, cream, milk, and butter. Cook for 6 to 7 hours low, stirring every few hours, until the grains are cooked through and soft.

Stir in the cheddar cheese, season to taste with salt and pepper, and serve.

Manhattan, Kansas   MAKES 2 CUPS

1 cup bourbon, such as W.L. Weller Special Reserve

1 cup Dolin Rouge vermouth

1 teaspoon Angostura bitters

1 Jonathan or Braeburn apple, sliced ¼ inch thick

4 whole cloves

2 sticks cinnamon

1 teaspoon cardamom pods

Ice cubes, for serving

Preheat the oven to 325°F. In a large bowl, combine the bourbon, vermouth, bitters, and apple slices. Place the cloves, cinnamon sticks, and cardamom pods on a baking sheet and toast in the oven for 8 to 10 minutes, until aromatic. Transfer the hot toasted spices to the bourbon mixture; cover. Chill the mixture overnight, or preferably for 3 days.

Using a fine-mesh sieve, strain the mixture into a pitcher. To serve, pour 3 ounces of the bourbon mixture into a rocks glass and top with ice cubes.

We had a small vegetable garden in our backyard when I was young. My sister and I were allowed to choose a vegetable every spring to plant next to the tomatoes, okra, and herbs my parents used to grow. My sister always picked cucumbers and I always picked carrots—even though I hated cooked carrots! This recipe would have probably changed my mind. We use heirloom carrots, which are smaller and sweeter than regular carrots, and they come in a variety of colors, which give the dish wonderful visual appeal. ★ C.G.

CARROTS

- 2 tablespoons vegetable oil
- 2 pounds small multicolored heirloom carrots, sliced ¼ inch thick on the diagonal
- 2 medium shallots, minced
- 4 cloves garlic, minced
- ½ cup chicken stock
- ¾ cup firmly packed light brown sugar
- 1 tablespoon apple cider vinegar
- 3 tablespoons unsalted butter

CRUMBLE

- ½ cup chopped carrot tops
- ½ cup chopped fresh flat-leaf parsley
- ½ cup panko bread crumbs
- 1 clove garlic, coarsely chopped
- 1 tablespoon extra-virgin olive oil

DUTCH OVEN-ROASTED CARROTS WITH BROWN SUGAR AND CARROT TOP CRUMBLE

For the carrots, heat the oil in a 2-quart Dutch oven over medium heat. When the oil is hot, add the carrots and brown on all sides until golden, 3 to 4 minutes.

Add the shallots and garlic and cook until translucent, about 2 minutes. Add the stock, brown sugar, and vinegar and cook until the liquid is reduced by half, about 6 minutes. Turn off the heat, add the butter, and stir until melted.

For the crumble, place the carrot tops, parsley, panko, and garlic in a food processor; blend well. With the processor running, slowly drizzle in the olive oil. Blend for 5 to 10 more seconds, until the crumbs are green and moist. Sprinkle the crumble over the carrots and serve.

CIDER-BRAISED BRISKET

SERVES 6

I miss my favorite barbecue dishes in the colder months, so I like to braise tougher cuts of meat in the Dutch oven. Ribs, brisket, or pork shoulder take on such a different flavor and texture when they come out of the oven—they're softer, more tender, and comforting. This brisket gets a nice fermented kick from the hard cider, and the flavors are intensified by the brisket being refrigerated overnight. ★ C.G.

⅓ cup vegetable oil

1 (5-pound) beef brisket, trimmed but with some fat remaining (see Note)

2 large yellow onions, sliced ¼ inch thick

6 cloves garlic, chopped

1 tablespoon tomato paste

2 tablespoons unbleached all-purpose flour

4 cups hard cider

2 cups chicken stock

2 sprigs fresh thyme

1 dried bay leaf

Preheat the oven to 300°F. Heat the oil over medium-high heat in a large (4- to 6-quart) Dutch oven. Place the brisket in the Dutch oven and sear on all sides until golden, about 5 minutes per side. Remove the brisket and set it on a plate. Remove all but 1 tablespoon of the fat from the Dutch oven. Add the onions, garlic, and tomato paste and cook over medium-high heat, stirring occasionally, until the onions are softened and golden, 10 to 12 minutes. Sprinkle the flour over the onions and cook, stirring constantly, until well combined, about 2 minutes. Add the cider, stock, thyme, and bay leaf, stirring to scrape up the browned bits from the pan, and bring to a simmer. Simmer for about 5 minutes to thicken the liquid. Add the brisket back to the Dutch oven.

Transfer the Dutch oven to the oven and cook the brisket for 4 hours, or until the brisket is fork-tender. Transfer the brisket to a large bowl; set a mesh strainer over the bowl and strain the sauce over the brisket. Discard the bay leaf and thyme sprigs, and transfer the onions to a small bowl. Cover both bowls with plastic wrap, poke holes in the plastic wrap to vent, and refrigerate overnight.

To serve, preheat the oven to 350°F. Remove any hardened fat from the top of the sauce and brisket. Place the brisket on a cutting board and slice into ¼-inch-thick slices. Arrange the slices in a 9 by 13-inch baking dish. Reserve ½ cup of the sauce, and pour the remaining sauce over the brisket. Cover the baking dish with aluminum foil, and heat in the oven for 20 to 30 minutes, until hot.

Meanwhile, put the onions and the reserved ½ cup sauce into a small sauce pan and bring to a simmer; let simmer for about 6 minutes. Serve the brisket slices with spoonfuls of onions and sauce alongside.

Ask your butcher to trim the brisket for braising, but be sure to ask for a little fat to be left on the meat. Often grocery store butchers trim too much, and you want some of that fat for flavor.

SERVES 4

The sweetness of roasted onions is always a treat during the cold winter months. With a little fresh goat cheese and ham, along with briny capers, this is an excellent side dish served next to a nice braised meat, such as Cider-Braised Brisket (page 60). ★ C.G.

- 2 large yellow onions
- Kosher salt and freshly ground black pepper
- 2 tablespoons vegetable oil
- ½ cup fresh goat cheese
- 4 tablespoons (½ stick) unsalted butter, softened
- 4 cloves garlic, peeled
- 2 tablespoons finely minced country ham
- 1 tablespoon minced capers
- 2 lemons, halved
- 2 tablespoons chopped fresh flat-leaf parsley

CAST IRON–ROASTED ONIONS WITH COUNTRY HAM, CAPERS, AND GOAT CHEESE

Preheat the oven to 425°F. Slice both onions in half from point to root, but keep the skin intact. Using a spoon, remove and discard the innermost 3 or 4 layers from the core of each onion half. Using a sharp knife, make crosshatch cuts on the cut side of each onion half. Season the onions with salt and pepper.

In a medium cast-iron pan over medium-high heat, heat the oil until it simmers. Add the onions, cut side down, and cook for about 4 minutes, or until well caramelized. Remove from the heat and set aside.

In a stand mixer fitted with the paddle attachment, whip the goat cheese and the butter for 5 minutes, or until soft and light. Scrape the sides of the bowl and place the butter and cheese mixture in a small bowl. Using a Microplane grater, finely grate the garlic cloves over the cheese mixture. Add a pinch of salt and a few turns of pepper. Add the ham and capers and stir to combine.

Remove the oil from the cast-iron pan and turn the onions skin side down in the pan. Rub the cheese mixture on the caramelized sides of the onions, making sure to spread the cheese between the layers of the onions. Place the pan in the oven and bake for 35 to 40 minutes, until the onions are soft. Transfer the onions to a serving plate. Remove the outer skins, squeeze a lemon half over each onion half, sprinkle with the parsley, and serve.

FOUR

From the Grill

Cooking outdoors is one of the best ways many Americans spend time with family and friends. I love nothing more than to have the lawn mowed and the "honey-dos" done so that I can open a cold beer and get the flames going. I cook three different ways outside: over an open flame in a fire pit, over coals on the grill, and in the smoker. We have a large fire pit in our backyard that is a blast to use when we're entertaining or cooking a large piece of meat like a leg of lamb, rack of pork, or even a whole fish. But it's not easy to control the heat, and open flames are less forgiving if you make a mistake. So in this chapter we'll focus on grilling and smoking.

Cooking on a grill over hot coals is the easiest and most consistent method, because you can control the heat level. This is best for cooking quick meals—burgers, chops, kebabs, vegetables, tender steaks like Worcestershire-Grilled Rib Eye (page 71), and fish like Grill-Roasted Walleye (page 87) are all great choices. Just make sure you purchase a good-quality cooker with a very thick skin. Heavy-gauge steel is important for maintaining heat and reducing flare-ups.

I always use a charcoal grill. It lends a flavor that a gas grill can never achieve. Plus, it's fun! Learning how to start and control a fire will make you a better cook in the long run. Gas grilling is fine, if that's what you prefer; it's certainly easier to fire it up and to control the heat. Whichever you choose, just keep it clean. A dirty grill and dirty grates make it tougher to cook because the food will stick to the grates.

If using a charcoal grill, I always use briquettes. They are much more consistent and they burn better and hotter for longer. You can add wood from time to time for smoke flavor if you're grilling, but remember that wood can catch fire, so keep it away from direct contact with the food.

Thermometers are an absolute necessity. Make sure your grill has a built-in thermometer to gauge the temperature of the grill, and use an instant-read meat thermometer to check the internal temperature of the meat. Here's how to get going on a charcoal grill:

1. When firing up a grill, open the dampers (vents) halfway. You want to get your fire hot, then use the dampers as you use the knobs on your stove: to increase or decrease the heat. When you close the dampers, there's less air to fuel the fire, so it cools down; this can also prevent flare-ups. More air equals more heat.

2. Fill a charcoal chimney with charcoal and light it. After about 15 minutes, the coals should be red- and white-hot. Carefully pour the coals into your grill. I like to start with a layer of coals that are white-hot, then add a small amount of fresh coals about 5 minutes before I cook.

3. Place the well-oiled grate at least 6 inches above the coals—you need space between your food and the coals.

4. When you have a good solid bed of heat, place your meat on the grill, then close the lid and your grill will act like an oven. This is where having heavy-grade steel helps with the radiant heat. If you have a good bed of coals, the fire will stay hot for an extended time even with the dampers closed down.

5. Move your food around on the grill to prevent flare-ups. Don't use a spray bottle of water on flare-ups with a charcoal grill—you'll end up spraying ash into the air and onto your food. (If you're using a gas grill, spray bottles can be useful.) I use the dampers and the weight of the grill to battle flare-ups. It's more effective and the least intrusive.

Smoking is a different beast. "Low and slow" is the name of the game here—cooking food, especially tougher cuts of meat, slowly at a low temperature. Smoked Brisket (page 81) is a perfect example: Smoked slowly for hours and hours, it becomes irresistibly tender and succulent.

The same rules apply to the smoker as to the grill: You want heavy-grade steel that keeps the heat inside. In our part of the country, we put everything in the smoker—beef, pork, lamb, poultry, game, and even vegetables. Rich, smoky, and spicy barbecue, of course, is the ultimate American food cooked in a smoker, and it's the food I've been steeped in practically since birth. This is how every red-blooded guy I know learned to cook.

See page 76 for more information on cooking barbecue, then sink your teeth into BBQ Spareribs (page 79) and Pulled Pork Sandwiches (82). You'll be an honorary KC barbecue master in no time. ★C.G.

TENDER CUTS

Tender cuts of beef or pork are the easiest meats to cook. You don't have to worry about the texture, but you do have to worry about flavor. Beef tenderloin, for instance, is a very tender piece of meat, but because it's very lean it doesn't have much flavor. Not only that, but it is also the most expensive piece of beef: On a 1,500-pound cow, the tenderloin weighs between 5 and 7 pounds. I prefer a good rib eye or Kansas City strip if I'm going to eat a tender cut.

Dry-aged cuts of beef are also prized for their tenderness and flavor. Dry aging is the process of holding beef uncovered in a refrigerated environment and allowing it to age under a watchful eye. During this process, the muscle tissue breaks down and the meat shrinks, concentrating the flavor. (Unfortunately the outside of the meat also decays, making it unattractive in a meat case at the grocery store. So you will likely need to special-order dry-aged beef.) Most good pieces of meat are aged for 21 days, but some restaurants will age their meat for up to 40 to 60 days. One restaurant I know ages its meat for up to 140 days, but that's just showing off. This time-consuming process results in outlandish prices, because a dry-aged piece of meat has lost moisture and gotten smaller, so it ends up costing more per pound.

Grill cooking is not an exact science, and cooking tender cuts of meat takes some skill and experience. It's nothing to be afraid of, but time and understanding go a long way. Meat is expensive, so it is important to pay attention!

Use an instant-read thermometer to make sure your steak is done the way you like it. To cook a rare steak with good char, take it off the grill when the temperature reaches 115° to 120°F. Medium-rare: 125° to 128°F. Medium: 128° to 132°F. Medium-well: 135° to 140°F. Well done: 140°F. Remember that the steaks will continue to cook after you remove them from the grill.

There's an age-old argument about the difference between a Kansas City strip steak and a New York strip. Some say it depends on whether there's a bone or not; others say it has to do with how much it's trimmed. And still others say that some New York chefs just didn't like the name "Kansas City" attached to such a great piece of meat. I simply call it delicious. This cut of steak doesn't need much help. A little herb, garlic, and olive oil and it's wonderful. Serve with Crispy Fried Eggplant (page 101) or Pickled Radishes (page 41)—or both. ★ C.G.

★ ★ ★ ★ ★ ★ ★

½ cup kosher salt

1 tablespoon freshly ground black pepper

6 cloves garlic, peeled

6 sprigs thyme

2 tablespoons extra-virgin olive oil

4 (12-ounce) Kansas City steaks

GRILLED GARLIC-THYME KANSAS CITY STRIP STEAKS

Place the salt, pepper, garlic, thyme, and olive oil in the bowl of a food processer and process until it forms a paste. Rub the steaks vigorously with the paste and let stand until the steaks come to room temperature.

If using a gas grill, turn it on high. If using charcoal, light the coals according to the directions on page 64 and place a well-oiled grate over the hot coals. Close the lid until the internal temperature reaches 400°F.

Place the meat on the hottest part of the grill and close the lid. Cook the steaks for 4 minutes, then rotate them 45 degrees. Close the lid and cook for another 2 minutes. Flip the steaks, close the lid, and cook for another 4 minutes. Rotate the steaks 45 degrees and cook for another 2 minutes, or until an instant-read thermometer registers the temperature for your desired doneness (see page 65). Let the meat rest for 3 to 4 minutes before serving to allow the juices to emerge from the center.

Paloma Shrub

¼ teaspoon Himalayan pink salt

Lemon or lime, sliced, for rimming the glass

Ice cubes

1½ ounces Espolòn Blanco tequila

3 ounces Grapefruit Shrub (recipe follows)

Rim a Collins glass with the pink salt. Place the salt on a shallow plate, run a sliced lime or lemon around the rim, and gently dip the glass rim into the salt, turning the glass in one direction until the rim is completely coated in a thin layer of salt. Fill the glass with ice cubes. Pour the tequila and shrub over the ice, stir, and serve.

Grapefruit Shrub — Makes 3 cups

Peels and strained juice from 3 grapefruits (about 2 cups juice)

¼ cup sugar

⅔ cup champagne vinegar

⅓ cup agave nectar syrup

⅛ teaspoon cayenne pepper

Place the grapefruit peels and sugar in a large bowl. Using a heavy wooden spoon, muddle the peels and sugar, pressing gently to release the citrus oil, about 3 minutes. Cover the bowl with plastic wrap and allow the sugar and grapefruit peels to sit overnight at room temperature.

Add the grapefruit juice, vinegar, agave nectar, and cayenne to the bowl. Whisk the ingredients to combine and to dissolve the sugar. Using a fine-mesh sieve, strain the grapefruit mixture into a large bowl and refrigerate until ready to serve. The grapefruit shrub will keep in an airtight container in the refrigerator for up to 3 weeks.

GRILLED T-BONES WITH RED WINE– ROSEMARY MARINADE

★ SERVES 4 ★

I call T-bones and porterhouse steaks "man steaks!" You get the best of both worlds: filet mignon on one side and Kansas City strip on the other. Both these steaks come from the short loin of the beef. The porterhouse is larger and has the proportionate part of the tenderloin. This is another great piece for dry aging, so ask if your butcher can get them for you. This steak would go nicely with the Dutch Oven–Roasted Carrots with Brown Sugar and Carrot Top Crumble on page 59 or the Slow Cooker Grits on page 58. ★ C.G.

½ cup kosher salt

¼ cup red wine (any kind will do)

2 tablespoons Worcestershire sauce

2 tablespoons freshly ground black pepper

2 tablespoons chopped fresh rosemary

1 tablespoon crushed red pepper flakes

1 tablespoon red wine vinegar

4 teaspoons paprika

4 cloves garlic, smashed and chopped

4 (1¼-pound) T-bone steaks

In a large shallow bowl, mix the salt, red wine, Worcestershire sauce, black pepper, rosemary, red pepper flakes, vinegar, paprika, and garlic. Whisk well. Add the steaks to the bowl and marinate, covered, in the refrigerator for at least 4 hours.

Remove from the refrigerator and discard the brine. Let the steaks come to room temperature before grilling.

If using a gas grill, turn it on high. If using charcoal, light the coals according to the instructions on page 64 and place a well-oiled grate over the hot coals. Close the lid until the internal temperature reaches 400°F.

Place the meat on the hottest part of the grill and close the lid. Cook the steaks for 4 minutes, then rotate them 45 degrees. Close the lid and cook for another 2 minutes. Flip the steaks, close the lid, and cook for another 4 minutes. Rotate the steaks 45 degrees and cook for another 2 minutes, or until an instant-read thermometer registers the temperature for your desired doneness (see page 65). Let the meat rest for 3 to 4 minutes before serving, to allow the juices to emerge from the center.

WORCESTERSHIRE-*Grilled* RIB EYE

SERVES 4

With its marbling and flavor, the rib eye is far and away my favorite cut of meat. It's rich, fatty, and such a treat. Roasting the whole short loin (where the rib eye comes from) results in the fabled prime rib. Megan and I love the taste of table steak sauces—we could be in the finest steak house in America, and Meg will embarrass me by asking for A.1. So we took the flavors we love in some of those sauces and made them into a marinade to penetrate the meat and give it great flavor. ★ C.G.

½ cup kosher salt
6 cloves garlic, peeled
4 sprigs oregano
Freshly grated zest of 1 lemon
2 tablespoons Worcestershire sauce
1 tablespoon extra-virgin olive oil
½ tablespoon red wine vinegar
4 (12-ounce) rib-eye steaks

Place the salt, garlic, oregano, and lemon zest in the bowl of a food processer and process until finely ground. In a small bowl, whisk together the Worcestershire sauce, oil, and vinegar. With the food processer running, add the liquid to make a paste. Rub the steaks vigorously with the paste and let stand until the steaks come to room temperature.

If using a gas grill, turn it on high. If using charcoal, light the coals according to the directions on page 64 and place a well-oiled grate over the hot coals. Close the lid until the internal temperature reaches 400°F.

Place the meat on the hottest part of the grill and close the lid. Cook the steaks for 4 minutes, then rotate them 45 degrees. Close the lid and cook for another 2 minutes. Flip the steaks, close the lid, and cook for another 4 minutes. Rotate them 45 degrees and cook for another 2 minutes, or until an instant-read thermometer registers the temperature for your desired doneness (see page 65). Let the meat rest for 3 to 4 minutes before serving, to allow the juices to emerge from the center.

WHAT'S COOKING

SEMI-TOUGH CUTS

These cuts of meat have a much better flavor profile because they generally have more fat and connective tissue, which are very tasty when they melt or break down. But these cuts are also much more difficult to cook. If you don't like to chew a lot, you have to find different methods for tenderizing the meat. A Jaccard tenderizer has a number of small blades to cut through the tough tissue. Just be aware that poking thousands of tiny holes in your meat can result in moisture loss. Cooking methods such as braising or *sous vide*—in a vacuum-sealed package, as we do in the restaurants—can help add back that moisture.

If you're cooking on a grill, you'll want to use a marinade, brine, or cure that helps break down the connective tissue and adds moisture to the meat. Personally, I like a steak that I can chew on and taste. The following are my favorites.

GRILLED FLATIRON STEAK WITH HORSERADISH-CIDER MARINADE

SERVES 4

The flatiron is a relatively new cut being used in restaurants: It comes from the top blade or shoulder of the cow. It is very difficult to butcher correctly, so ask your butcher to cut it for you. It's wonderfully marbled and has some good chew to it. You can use some of the techniques I describe on page 72 to tenderize the steak, such as a Jaccard device. If flatiron is difficult to find, hanger steak is also great with this marinade, which gets a sweet-spicy kick from the honey, mustard, and horseradish. This steak would be great with Cast Iron–Roasted Onions with Country Ham, Capers, and Goat Cheese (page 61) or Slow-Cooked Pale Ale Barley (page 53). ★ C.G.

1 cup apple cider vinegar
½ cup extra-virgin olive oil
⅓ cup Dijon mustard
¼ cup honey
3 tablespoons prepared horseradish
4 cloves garlic, grated on a Microplane
4 (8-ounce) flatiron steaks

In a medium bowl, mix the vinegar, oil, mustard, honey, horseradish, and garlic. Arrange the steaks in a large casserole dish and pour the marinade over them. Cover with the lid or wrap with plastic wrap and refrigerate overnight.

Remove the steaks from the refrigerator and discard the marinade. Let the steaks come to room temperature before grilling.

If using a gas grill, turn it on high. If using charcoal, light the coals according to the directions on page 64 and place a well-oiled grate over the hot coals. Close the lid until the internal temperature reaches 400°F.

Place the meat on the hottest part of the grill and close the lid. Cook the steaks for 4 minutes, then rotate them 45 degrees. Close the lid and cook for another 2 minutes. Flip the steaks, close the lid, and cook for another 4 minutes. Rotate the steaks 45 degrees and cook for another 2 minutes, or until an instant-read thermometer registers the temperature for your desired doneness (see page 65). Allow the meat to rest for 3 to 4 minutes before serving, to allow the juices to emerge from the center.

HANGER STEAK *with* HERBED GARLIC-CAPER SAUCE

SERVES 4

Hanger steak used to be known as the butcher's steak, because butchers commonly tossed it aside to be ground later—or took it home for their own dinner. Today it's one of the most popular cuts of beef, because it's fairly lean, reasonably priced, and full of flavor. In fact, this steak has so much flavor that you can really get aggressive with seasonings. The garlic, lemon, and capers in this South American–style marinade are able to stand up to the richness of the meat. Serve this with crispy Fried Okra (page 99) or Quick Pickles (page 37). ★ C.G.

3 bunches flat-leaf parsley, stemmed and chopped
⅓ cup water
⅓ cup sherry vinegar
2 tablespoons drained capers
5 garlic cloves, peeled
¼ teaspoon kosher salt
¼ teaspoon freshly ground white pepper
½ cup extra-virgin olive oil
4 (6-ounce) hanger steaks

Place the parsley, water, vinegar, capers, garlic, salt, and pepper in a blender. Purée on high speed and, with the blender running, slowly add the olive oil. Pour the mixture into a small bowl. Reserve 4 tablespoons of the sauce for serving. Rub the hanger steaks generously with the remainder of the sauce, shaking off any excess.

If using a gas grill, turn it on high. If using charcoal, light the coals according to the directions on page 64 and place a well-oiled grate over the hot coals. Close the lid until the temperature reaches 400°F.

Place the meat on the hottest part of the grill and close the lid. Cook the steaks for 2 minutes, then rotate them 45 degrees. Close the lid and cook for another 2 minutes. Flip the steaks, close the lid, and cook for another 2 minutes. Rotate the steaks 45 degrees and cook for another 2 minutes, or until an instant-read thermometer registers the temperature for your desired doneness (see page 65). Let the meat rest for 3 to 4 minutes before serving, to allow the juices to emerge from the center. Serve each steak with 1 tablespoon of the reserved sauce on top.

Grilled Flank Steak
with Soy-Brown Sugar Marinade

★ **SERVES 4** ★

Flank steak was a cut that ended up on our table often when I was a kid. It was cheap, so my parents liked it; I loved how the ends got crisp on the thin tail of the steak. Since flank steak is a tougher cut, you'll want to use some of the techniques described on page 72 to tenderize the steak, such as a Jaccard device. Then marinate it overnight in this great marinade to tenderize it further. The sugar in the marinade will caramelize on the grill. Serve this with Pickled Radishes (page 41). ★ C.G.

1 cup balsamic vinegar

⅓ cup soy sauce

¼ cup firmly packed light brown sugar

4 cloves garlic, grated on a Microplane

1 tablespoon kosher salt

1 tablespoon sambal oelek (see Note)

1 teaspoon Old Bay Seasoning

1 teaspoon ground mustard

1 (2-pound) flank steak

In a medium shallow bowl, mix the vinegar, soy sauce, brown sugar, garlic, salt, *sambal oelek*, Old Bay, and ground mustard. Add the flank steak to the bowl and marinate, covered, in the refrigerator for at least 4 hours.

Remove from the refrigerator. Let the steak come to room temperature before grilling.

If using a gas grill, turn it on high. If using charcoal, light the coals according to the directions on page 64 and place a well-oiled grate over the hot coals. Close the lid until the internal temperature reaches 400°F.

Place the meat on the hottest part of the grill and close the lid. Cook the steak for 2 minutes, then rotate it 45 degrees. Close the lid and cook for another 2 minutes. Flip the steak, close the lid, and cook for another 2 minutes. Rotate the steak 45 degrees and cook for another 2 minutes, or until an instant-read thermometer registers the temperature for your desired doneness (see page 65). Let the meat rest for 3 to 4 minutes before serving, to allow the juices to emerge from the center. Slice against the grain along the long side of the steak and serve on a platter.

Sambal oelek is a spicy red chili pepper sauce found at some supermarkets and in Asian grocery stores.

WHAT'S COOKING

BARBECUE

For me, smoking meat is a passion. So I want equipment that's dedicated to the job. Most people have a grill in their backyard or garage, and yes, you can use a grill as a smoker. But I would rather have a smoker I can grill on than a grill I can smoke in. You need room for a smoker, lots of it. And having a cooker that can fill with good smoke and a fire that is easy to access will make your life a lot easier.

Follow the manufacturer's directions for firing up your smoker. All smokers are different, and you're going to have to watch your fire, feed it fuel, work the dampers, and alternate between charcoal and wood. This takes a little finesse and knowledge of your smoker that comes from using it repeatedly. But the tender, smoky, juicy results are so worth it.

BBQ SPARERIBS

★ SERVES 4 ★

Ribs are what started it all for me—I got launched on my whole career because I wanted to know how to cook ribs. And my curiosity took me on the journey I'm still on. Here's what I learned along the way: Ribs take practice and patience. You should resist the urge to finish them inside in your kitchen oven. Your smoker *is* an oven—you just need to figure out how to make it act that way. It's a dry, slow heat source that also requires moisture to coax out the tenderness in the meat. You can achieve that by wrapping the ribs in foil, or placing a foil pan filled halfway with water under the grate (this also serves to catch the drips, preventing flare-ups). I love to slip the meat off properly cooked pork ribs—when the bones turn white, you know they're done right. ★ C.G.

1 (3 to 4-pound) slab pork spareribs
1 cup BBQ Dry Rub (page 30)
¼ cup molasses
¼ cup firmly packed light brown sugar
1 cup BBQ Sauce (page 26)

Let the ribs sit at room temperature for 30 minutes. Rub them all over with the dry rub.

Fire up your smoker according to the manufacturer's directions and bring the temperature to 250°F.

Place the ribs in the smoker and close the lid. Watching the fire, feeding the fuel, and working the dampers as needed to keep the smoker temperature at 250°F, cook the ribs for 2 hours, or until an instant-read thermometer registers an internal temperature of 160°F.

Remove the pork from the smoker and rub all over with the molasses, then the brown sugar. Wrap the ribs in heavy-duty aluminum foil and cook in the smoker for another 2 hours, or until the meat starts to pull slightly from the bone and the internal temperature reaches 195°F. Serve with the barbecue sauce alongside.

SMOKED BRISKET

Serves 10 to 12

Brisket is barbecued only in the middle of America, from Texas north to Kansas City. As a matter of fact, that's all Texas barbecue is. And they do it well. So well that they think everyone else is terrible at it. But barbecuing brisket is not rocket science. It just takes patience—a lot of patience. If you're planning on serving brisket, be ready to get up very early or to stay up all night! And wait until you've got a good crowd coming—this recipe makes a lot of brisket, and you don't want any going to waste. Be sure to cut off and save the burnt ends of the brisket for use in the Spicy Tomato and Burnt-Ends Hash with Fried Eggs (page 3). ★ C.G.

1 (8 to 10-pound) beef brisket
2 cups BBQ Dry Rub (page 30)
3 cups BBQ Sauce (page 26)

Let the brisket sit at room temperature for 1 hour. Rub the brisket all over with the dry rub. Fire up your smoker according to the manufacturer's instructions and bring the temperature to 250°F.

Place the brisket fat side down in the smoker and close the lid. Watching the fire, feeding the fuel, and working the dampers as needed to keep the smoker temperature at 250°F, cook for 5 hours.

Flip the brisket and cook for another 5 to 8 hours, until an instant-read thermometer registers an internal temperature of 195°F. Remove the brisket from the smoker and let it rest for 1 hour.

Trim off and save the burnt ends from the front and back of the brisket, for use in the Spicy Tomato and Burnt-Ends Hash with Fried Eggs (page 3). Carefully slice the brisket, brush with the barbecue sauce, and serve.

PULLED PORK SANDWICHES

★ ★ ★ ★ ★ ★ ★

SERVES 6 TO 8

Pork butt, aka pork shoulder, is the common theme throughout most of the barbecue world. We all may use different sauces, or no sauce at all, but most barbecue cultures agree that pork butt is a staple. Here in KC, pulled pork sandwiches reign supreme, and all the good barbecue joints argue about who has the best one. Obviously, we do! We serve them at both of our restaurants, and this is how we do it. ★ C.G.

1 (5-pound) bone-in pork butt
2 cups BBQ Dry Rub (page 30)
⅓ cup molasses
⅓ cup firmly packed light brown sugar
Hamburger buns, for serving
2 cups BBQ Sauce (page 26)

Let the pork shoulder sit at room temperature for 1 hour. Rub generously with the dry rub. Fire up your smoker according to the manufacturer's instructions and bring the temperature to 250°F.

Place the pork in the smoker and close the lid. Watching the fire, feeding the fuel, and working the dampers as needed to keep the smoker temperature at 250°F, cook the pork for about 3 hours, or until an instant-read thermometer registers an internal temperature of 160°F.

Rub the pork all over with the molasses, then the brown sugar. Wrap well in heavy-duty aluminum foil and cook for another 3 to 4 hours, until the internal temperature of the pork reaches 195°F. Pull from the smoker and let rest for 1 hour.

Using forks or pork claws, shred the meat. Serve on hamburger buns with the barbecue sauce.

FISH

Fish is very delicate, so I only cook whole fish directly on the grill. If I am working with fish fillets, I usually cook them in a cast-iron pan on a grill or open fire. For me, this is reminiscent of the "tinfoil dinners" I loved when I was a kid on camping trips. We'd catch fish; fillet them; wrap them up in aluminum foil with some vegetables, herbs, and butter; and put them on a bed of coals by the campfire. In 10 minutes, we'd have a hot, fresh, tasty dinner. Working with a cast-iron pan on the grill is no different—it's just a little safer. You still get the wood-smoked taste, but you get the texture and control of fish cooked in a pan.

SERVES 4

Trout is an amazing freshwater fish. Not only is it delicious, but it's also so much fun to fish for. I used to fly-fish with my grandfather when I was little. I had a hard time getting the hang of it, but I loved spending time with him. I still have all his gear to this day. These days I'm more likely to catch my trout at the fish market, but I cook it in the great outdoors and think of my grandfather. Serve this dish with Yukon Gold Potato Salad with Summer Corn, Country Ham, and Garlicky Lemon-Chive Dressing (page 45). ★ C.G.

4 (6-ounce) skin-on trout fillets

Kosher salt and freshly ground black pepper

4 tablespoons (½ stick) unsalted butter, softened

2 sprigs thyme

2 sprigs tarragon

4 cloves garlic, thinly sliced

2 lemons, peeled and halved (peels reserved)

GRILLED TROUT
WITH TARRAGON, THYME,
AND LEMON

If using a gas grill, turn it on medium-low. If using charcoal, light the coals according to the directions on page 64 and place a well-oiled grate over the hot coals. Close the lid until the internal temperature reaches 275°F.

Season the trout with salt and pepper. Set a large cast-iron pan on the grill. Add the butter and immediately add the fish, flesh side down, along with the thyme, tarragon, garlic, and lemon peels. Close the lid and cook for 8 minutes, or until the flesh is opaque. Remove the pan from the grill, and squeeze the lemon halves over the fish. Serve immediately.

GRILLED PERCH WITH LEEKS, HERBS, AND LIME

SERVES 4

Perch is a relative of walleye but much smaller, so it doesn't require much cooking time. It has a very light and mild flavor, and it is also great fried. If you catch your own perch, you'll have some butchering to do, but nothing's better than cleaning fish by the fire. Then just cook them up with a little olive oil, lime, leeks, and herbs, and these little guys are great. ★ C.G.

8 (3-ounce) perch fillets
Kosher salt and freshly ground black pepper
3 tablespoons extra-virgin olive oil
2 leeks, sliced (white part only)
4 cloves garlic, thinly sliced
4 sprigs oregano
2 dried bay leaves
1 lime, halved

If using a gas grill, turn it on medium-low. If using charcoal, light the coals according to the directions on page 64 and place a well-oiled grate over the hot coals. Close the lid until the internal temperature reaches 275°F.

Season the perch with salt and pepper. Place a large cast-iron pan on the grill. Add the olive oil, leeks, and garlic. Season to taste with salt and pepper and cook for 4 minutes, or until the leeks start to become tender. Add the fish, oregano, and bay leaves. Close the lid and cook for 6 minutes or until the flesh is opaque. Remove the pan from the grill, discard the bay leaves, squeeze the lime halves over the fish, and serve.

GRILL-ROASTED WALLEYE

★ ★ ★ ★ ★ ★ ★ ★ ★

SERVES 4

Walleye is a large freshwater fish that comes from the northern Midwest. Megan grew up eating this fish from the Great Lakes, and we love it at home. It's a large fish, so the fillets are an excellent size, similar to ocean fish. If you can't find it, you can use any similar large flaky fish, like halibut or salmon. Walleye has a mild flavor and you can prepare it many ways, but we like the classic accompaniments: onion, garlic, lemon, and white wine—plus Quick Pickles (page 37) on the side. ★ C.G.

4 (6-ounce) walleye fillets

Kosher salt and freshly ground black pepper

3 tablespoons unsalted butter

1 small red onion, thinly sliced

4 cloves garlic, thinly sliced

Peel and juice of 1 lemon

1 teaspoon paprika

¼ cup dry white wine

If using a gas grill, turn it on high. If using charcoal, light the coals according to the directions on page 64 and place a well-oiled grate over the hot coals. Close the lid until the internal temperature reaches 400°F.

Season the walleye with salt and pepper. Set a medium cast-iron pan on the grill over a healthy bed of coals. Add 1 tablespoon of the butter to the pan. When it starts to bubble, add the walleye and cook for 1½ minutes. Add the onion, garlic, and lemon peel. Cook for another minute, flip the fish, and sprinkle with the paprika. Cook for another 30 seconds, then add the white wine and lemon juice. Close the grill lid and roast for 2 minutes, or until the internal temperature reaches 135°F. Add the remaining 2 tablespoons of butter and use a spoon to baste the fish until the butter is completely melted, about 30 seconds. Serve immediately.

FIVE
From the Fryer

The legendary fryer: No other piece of cooking equipment inspires so much scorn and so much craving at the same time. There's just something about a crispy golden crust on everything from chicken to green tomatoes that is absolutely irresistible.

Apple pie may be some people's standard of all-American eating, but for me, it's fried chicken. Didn't everyone grow up eating fried chicken—whether at diners or backyard picnics or under fireworks on the Fourth of July? It was certainly part of my childhood, and part of my father's childhood before that. In fact, the pans I fry in were my father's, and they came from his mother and father. Even though I never met my dad's mother, knowing that I'm cooking and eating from the same pans she used gives me as much comfort as the food that comes from them.

Frying food at home is laborious and messy. Maybe that's a good thing. This kind of eating should be a comforting luxury, not an everyday occurrence. When I was young and the frying pans came out, you knew dinner was going to be good. Today, when I'm planning a winter dinner party or a backyard get-together, I know there will be someone who can't eat fish or won't eat beef—but flour up some yard bird or dip some vegetables in batter and throw them into hot oil, and everyone will be happy.

A few tips on frying:

★ Peanut oil is best for frying because of the flavor it adds to the food, but if there are allergy issues, use canola oil.

★ Make sure the oil reaches the proper temperature before adding the food to it. If the oil is not hot enough, the food will absorb the oil instead, and all your hard work will be wasted.

★ For a perfectly crispy crust, work quickly and use a light touch when flouring the food: The food should have an even coating of the flour mixture, but be sure to shake off the excess. And never let the food sit in the flour mixture for more than 2 minutes, or you'll kill the chemical reaction that occurs between the flour, baking powder, and baking soda to create the crust.

Feel free to mix and match the Sauerkraut Sauce (page 105), Smoky Hot Sauce (page 103), and Caper-Horseradish Sauce (page 102) with any of the fried dishes in this chapter. They're all delicious. ★ C.G.

Garrelts FRIED CHICKEN

★ SERVES 4 ★

Fried chicken is the Holy Grail in our family—so much so that we built a restaurant around it. When I was young, we went to an old roadhouse chicken place called Boots & Coats. It was dark, dingy, and filled with cigarette smoke. We went there almost every Thursday night. They didn't take reservations, so we would wait for over an hour for a table—I can still remember watching the Hamm's beer clock on the wall. I spent years trying to create a fried chicken as good as the one I remember from Boots & Coats, and I've finally mastered it. Fried chicken can be a real pain to cook at home; almost everyone who attempts it complains that the chicken burns on the outside before it's finished on the inside. The trick is to use two pots of frying oil: one for the outside of the bird, with a high temperature to get that golden crust, and one for the inside, with the oil at a lower temperature to finish cooking the meat. Our fried chicken at Rye actually involves a 3-day process: We start by brining the chicken for 24 hours to keep it juicy, and for a superior crust we then dry the chicken uncovered in the refrigerator overnight. To cook as many fried chicken dinners as we do, it's necessary to follow this long method. But the much shorter method here creates a result that's just as delicious as the chicken we serve at the restaurants. ★ C.G.

BRINE

4 quarts water

¼ cup kosher salt

2 tablespoons freshly squeezed lemon juice

2 tablespoons sugar

2 tablespoons honey

2¼ teaspoons freshly ground black pepper

½ tablespoon finely grated lemon zest

15 whole cloves

4 cloves garlic, smashed

4 dried bay leaves

1 (3 to 4-pound) chicken, cut into 10 pieces

SLURRY

4 cups water

4 cups buttermilk (full-fat if you can find it)

1 cup unbleached all-purpose flour

6 large egg whites

2 tablespoons iodized salt

2 teaspoons freshly cracked black pepper

1 teaspoon garlic powder

1 teaspoon cayenne pepper

FLOUR MIX

3 cups unbleached all-purpose flour

3 tablespoons garlic powder

3 tablespoons onion powder

3 teaspoons kosher salt

2 teaspoons paprika

2 teaspoons cayenne pepper

½ teaspoon freshly cracked black pepper

Peanut or canola oil, for frying

White Gravy (page 6), for serving

Continued

For the brine, combine the water, salt, lemon juice, sugar, honey, pepper, lemon zest, cloves, garlic, and bay leaves in a large sauce pan and bring to a simmer. Remove from the stove and chill uncovered for 2 to 3 hours, until the liquid is below 40°F.

Place the chicken in a large deep casserole dish with a lid and pour the brine over it. Make sure the chicken is completely submerged. Refrigerate overnight.

Remove the chicken from the brine and lightly rinse the chicken. Pat dry with paper towels. Set aside.

For the slurry, place the water, buttermilk, flour, egg whites, salt, black pepper, garlic powder, and cayenne in a large bowl. Whisk well to incorporate. Set aside.

For the flour mix, place the flour, garlic powder, onion powder, salt, paprika, cayenne, and black pepper in a medium bowl. Mix well and set aside. Line a plate with paper towels or have a wire rack ready.

To fry the chicken, add enough oil to 2 medium Dutch ovens or deep cast-iron pans to reach halfway up the sides. Heat one over medium-high heat until an instant-read thermometer registers 375°F; heat the other over medium heat until the thermometer registers 315°F.

Working in batches, place the chicken in the slurry for 5 to 10 minutes. Working quickly with one piece at a time, dip the chicken in the flour mix and coat all sides. It's important that you work quickly so that the baking soda can react with the flour in the oil to give you a crispy crust. Do not let the chicken sit in the flour for more than 2 minutes. Using tongs, carefully put half of the chicken in the 375°F frying oil. Cook for 3 minutes, or until the chicken is golden brown. Using tongs, transfer the chicken pieces to the 315°F pot and cook for 15 to 18 minutes (do not to allow the oil temperature to dip below 300°F), until the internal temperature of the chicken reaches 165°F or above.

Set the finished chicken on the plate lined with paper towels or on a wire rack and repeat with the rest of the chicken. Serve with the white gravy.

CHICKEN-FRIED STEAK and GRAVY

SERVES 4

When I was a kid, we lived in a small town 30 miles north of Kansas City, and chicken-fried steak was a staple at every diner in the rural towns around us. It evolved from the German dish Wiener schnitzel, but it has become a quintessential American food. Now if I had to choose my last meal, this would be it. In fact, my last meal might be breakfast, because biscuits, gravy, and chicken-fried steak have always been my favorite breakfast foods. ★ C.G.

4 (5-ounce) cube steaks (or pounded and tenderized sirloin or top round)
Kosher salt and freshly ground black pepper
3 cups unbleached all-purpose flour
3 tablespoons BBQ Dry Rub (page 30)
1 teaspoon ground mustard
1 teaspoon garlic powder
1 cup buttermilk (full-fat if you can find it)
1 teaspoon baking powder
½ teaspoon baking soda
1 large egg
Peanut or canola oil, for frying
Sausage Gravy (page 8), for serving

Season the steaks well with salt and pepper and let rest at room temperature while you prepare the other ingredients.

In a medium casserole dish, whisk together the flour, dry rub, ground mustard, and garlic powder. In a large bowl, whisk together the buttermilk, baking powder, baking soda, and egg.

Line a tray with paper towels and set aside. In a large cast-iron skillet, heat 1 inch of oil to 375°F. Use a good instant-read thermometer and make sure the oil has reached 375°F before you go to the next step.

Unless you have a pan the size of Kansas, you'll have to do this in batches: Dredge one steak through the flour and shake off any extra flour—this is very important, as you want your crust to be light. Dip the floured steak into the buttermilk mixture, holding the steak with your fingertips above the bowl to let the extra buttermilk drain off. Then dip the steak back into the flour, and put it immediately into the hot oil. Do not wait or let the meat sit with the flour on it. Cook the steak in the hot oil for 2 minutes on one side. Flip and cook for another 2 minutes. Remove and place on the tray lined with paper towels. Repeat with the other steaks. Transfer the steaks to serving plates and top with the sausage gravy.

CORNMEAL-FRIED CATFISH

Catfish is a simple fish that is easily attainable in the Midwest, where we fish for them in ponds and lakes. (We avoid farm-raised catfish altogether; they're mostly fed pellets that are similar to dog food— so guess what the fish end up tasting like?) Both Meg and I grew up eating catfish: me when I would fish with my grandpa, and Meg when she would go to fish fries with her family. It's a flavorful fish that is especially good coated with cornmeal and fried. We usually eat whole fried catfish around here, but I used fillets in this recipe because they're probably easier to find. ★ C.G.

4 cups buttermilk (full-fat if you can find it)

¼ cup Hot Sauce (page 28) or store-bought

2 teaspoons kosher salt

3 teaspoons freshly ground black pepper

4 (4 to 5-ounce) catfish fillets

1½ cups yellow cornmeal

2 tablespoons cornstarch

1 tablespoon Old Bay Seasoning

2½ teaspoons baking powder

1 teaspoon garlic powder

1 teaspoon onion powder

½ teaspoon cayenne pepper

Peanut or canola oil, for frying

In a medium bowl, combine the buttermilk, hot sauce, salt, and 2 teaspoons of the black pepper. Add the catfish to the buttermilk mixture, cover, and refrigerate for 1 hour.

In a large bowl, combine the cornmeal, cornstarch, Old Bay, baking powder, garlic powder, onion powder, cayenne, and the remaining 1 teaspoon black pepper. Add enough oil to a 10-inch cast-iron skillet or Dutch oven to come a little less than halfway up the side of the skillet. Heat over medium heat until an instant-read thermometer registers 335°F. Line a tray with paper towels.

Pull each catfish fillet out of the buttermilk mixture and shake off any excess liquid. Dredge the catfish in the cornmeal mixture, shaking off he excess. Working with 2 fillets at a time, fry the catfish 3 to 4 minutes on each side, until golden brown and crispy. Transfer the fish to paper towels to drain.

State Fair

2 ounces Salted Corn Whiskey (recipe follows)

1 ounce sweet red vermouth, such as Carpano Antica Formula

1 tablespoon Caramel Simple Syrup (page 42)

Whiskey or water, for rimming the glass

¼ teaspoon ground Salted Toffee (recipe follows)

Ice cubes

In a cocktail shaker using a tall spoon, stir together the whiskey, vermouth, and caramel syrup. Rim a highball glass with salted toffee. Place the salted toffee on a shallow plate, run the whiskey around the rim, and gently dip the glass rim into the toffee, turning the glass in one direction until the rim is completely coated in a thin layer of toffee. Fill the glass with ice cubes. Pour the whiskey mixture over the ice and serve.

Salted Corn Whiskey   Makes 1½ cups

1 tablespoon canola oil
1 cup popcorn kernels
1 tablespoon unsalted butter, melted
¼ teaspoon kosher salt
3 cups whiskey

In a deep stockpot, combine the oil and corn kernels. Cover the pot with a sheet of aluminum foil and heat over high heat to pop the corn, 6 to 8 minutes, until the popping slows and stops and all the kernels have popped.

In a large bowl, stir together the melted butter and salt. Add the warm popped corn to the bowl and toss to evenly coat the popped corn with the butter and salt. Pour the whiskey over the buttered popcorn and stir with a wooden spoon to combine. Cover the bowl with plastic wrap and allow the mixture to infuse for 1 hour at room temperature.

Transfer the mixture to the freezer to allow the butter to set and float to the top of the whiskey, about 2 hours or preferably overnight.

Gently remove the firm butter from the top of the whiskey and discard. Strain the whiskey twice through a fine-mesh sieve lined with a coffee filter; discard the popcorn. Reserve the whiskey in an airtight container at room temperature until ready to use, up to 1 week.

Salted Toffee   Makes 2 cups

¾ cup (1½ sticks) unsalted butter, melted
1 cup sugar
2 tablespoons water
1½ tablespoons light corn syrup
1 teaspoon kosher salt

Line a baking sheet with a nonstick baking mat (such as a Silpat) and set aside. In a large sauce pan, stir together the melted butter, sugar, water, and corn syrup. Turn the heat to medium and, without stirring, heat the sugar mixture to 300°F on a candy thermometer. Carefully pour the caramelized sugar onto the prepared baking sheet. Let the toffee cool to room temperature so it can be handled and is not sticky.

Break the toffee into pieces and transfer to a food processor. Add the salt and pulse to grind the toffee to fine crumbs. Reserve the ground toffee in an airtight container at room temperature until ready to use, up to 1 week. The ground toffee can also be sprinkled on ice cream or tossed with toasted and salted nuts.

FRIED GREEN TOMATOES

★ ★ ★ ★ ★ ★

SERVES 6 TO 8

8 medium green tomatoes, sliced ¼ inch thick

Kosher salt and freshly ground black pepper

1 cup unbleached all-purpose flour

1 teaspoon ground mustard

1 teaspoon smoked paprika

1 cup buttermilk (full-fat if you can find it)

1 large egg

2 cups panko bread crumbs

Peanut or canola oil, for frying

Sauerkraut Sauce (page 105), for serving

In the South, where fried green tomatoes are a staple, tomatoes have a nice long growing season. Midwestern growing seasons are a roller-coaster ride, to say the least. We see monsoon rains followed by blasts of cold weather followed inevitably by a grass-scorching drought. The dry times always seem to hit the hardest in August and the first part of September. The tomatoes struggle during this time, and then in late September we'll get a late rainstorm and receive a bumper crop of green tomatoes. We pickle and fry these babies until the final fruit. While Midwestern fried green tomatoes may be similar in style to the Southern version, I like to think we cherish ours more because of all we go through to get them. ★ C.G.

Preheat the oven to 200°F. Line a baking sheet with paper towels and set aside.

Season the tomatoes with salt and pepper. Place the flour, ground mustard, and paprika in a medium bowl and mix well. Whisk together the buttermilk and egg in a second medium bowl. Place the panko in a third medium bowl.

Working with one tomato slice at a time, coat the tomatoes first in the flour mix (knocking off excess), then in the buttermilk and egg, then finally in the panko. Transfer the breaded slices to a baking sheet or tray.

Heat ¾ inch of oil in a medium skillet until an instant-read thermometer registers 350°F. Working in batches, fry the tomato slices for about 2 minutes per side, until golden brown. Using a slotted spoon, transfer the cooked tomatoes to the baking sheet lined with paper towels, and season with salt and pepper. Keep the cooked tomatoes in the preheated oven while you fry the remaining slices. Serve the tomatoes warm with the Sauerkraut Sauce or other dipping sauce.

FRIED OKRA

Serves 4

When I first started cooking, I went from being fascinated with French cooking to being fascinated with New Orleans cooking—it served as my first connection between European cooking and American cooking. That's when I started cooking with okra, although I didn't know what else to do with it besides putting it in gumbo or frying it. Fried okra is one of those great dishes that started in the South and made its way north. When my father and I are on our way home from the family farm, we'll often stop by a little watering hole outside of La Cygne, Kansas, for a couple cold beers and some fried okra. We grow some okra on our farm, and now we've started cooking it like this. Okra holds up well with a nice crust, and cooking it quickly avoids the sliminess that okra is (in)famous for. Plus, salty fried okra pairs well with beer! ★ C.G.

2 pounds fresh okra, sliced ½ inch thick

Kosher salt and freshly ground black pepper

½ cup buttermilk (full-fat if you can find it)

1 large egg

1 cup unbleached all-purpose flour

½ cup yellow cornmeal

2 tablespoons BBQ Dry Rub (page 30)

¼ teaspoon cayenne pepper

Peanut or canola oil, for frying

Smoky Hot Sauce (page 103), for serving

Season the okra with salt and pepper. In a medium bowl, whisk together the buttermilk and the egg. In another medium bowl, combine the flour, cornmeal, dry rub, and cayenne.

Pour enough oil into a medium Dutch oven to come one-third of the way up the sides. Heat the oil over medium-high heat until an instant-read thermometer registers 350°F. Line a plate with paper towels.

Dip the okra into the buttermilk-egg mixture, then dredge in the flour-cornmeal mixture to coat well. Using a slotted spoon, carefully slide the okra into the hot oil and cook for 2 to 4 minutes, until golden brown. Remove from the oil and transfer to the plate lined with paper towels to drain. Serve immediately with the Smoky Hot Sauce or other dipping sauce.

CRISPY FRIED
EGGPLANT
(OPPOSITE)

FRIED GREEN
TOMATOES
(PAGE 98)

FRIED OKRA
(PAGE 99)

CRISPY FRIED EGGPLANT

Eggplant can be a hard plant to love—it's spongy, weird-looking, and has a dumb name, and when Mom or Dad brought one home I always knew what I *wasn't* eating for dinner. But with a little coaxing, the eggplant can be meaty, tasty, and good for you. It is full of phytochemicals, which is good for fighting heart disease—but we're going to fry them, so just forget about that. ★ C.G.

1 eggplant (about 1 pound), cut crosswise into ½-inch-thick slices

Kosher salt and freshly ground black pepper

1 cup unbleached all-purpose flour

⅓ cup cornstarch

1 tablespoon garlic powder

2 teaspoons Old Bay Seasoning

1 teaspoon ground mustard

1 teaspoon smoked paprika

2 cups buttermilk (full-fat if you can find it)

1 large egg

2 cups panko bread crumbs

Peanut or canola oil, for frying

Caper-Horseradish Sauce (page 102), for serving

Set a wire rack over paper towels, and place the eggplant on the rack. Sprinkle both sides with salt and let sit for 1 hour to leach out the moisture. Gently rinse the eggplant, pat dry with paper towels, and season with black pepper (you do not need to add any more salt).

In a large bowl, whisk together the flour, cornstarch, garlic powder, Old Bay, ground mustard, and paprika. In a second large bowl, whisk together the buttermilk and the egg. Place the panko in a third large bowl.

Pour enough oil into a medium cast-iron pan to reach a depth of ½ inch. Heat the oil over medium-high heat until an instant-read thermometer registers 375°F. Line a baking sheet with paper towels and set aside.

Working with one eggplant slice at a time, dredge each slice in the flour mixture, coating it thoroughly and shaking off the excess. Dip the slice into the egg mixture to coat, then dredge it in the bread crumbs, pressing on the crumbs to make them adhere. Transfer the coated eggplant slice to paper towels and let it dry slightly. Using tongs, gently slide the breaded eggplant slice into the hot oil and fry for 1 minute on each side, or until golden brown. Transfer the slice to the prepared baking sheet to drain, and repeat with the remaining eggplant slices. Sprinkle the eggplant slices lightly with salt and serve with the Caper-Horseradish Sauce or other dipping sauce.

Caper-Horseradish Sauce

★ **MAKES ABOUT 2½ CUPS** ★

I love the old horseradish and sour cream sauce that is a staple with prime rib and shaved beef sandwiches. When I was young, this was an exotic sauce. Kick out the sour cream, add mayonnaise, capers, fresh herbs, and garlic, and you'll be smearing this version on cold cuts and anything fresh from the garden. This is delicious with Crispy Fried Eggplant (page 101), but it is a versatile sauce that can also be served with roasted meats or fish. ★ C.G.

2 cups mayonnaise

2 tablespoons chopped capers

2 tablespoons chopped fresh oregano

1 tablespoon plus 1 teaspoon prepared horseradish

2 cloves garlic, finely minced or pressed through a garlic press

Kosher salt and freshly ground black pepper

In a medium bowl, combine the mayonnaise, capers, oregano, horseradish, and garlic. Season with salt and pepper to taste, and mix well. Transfer to an airtight container and refrigerate until ready to serve. It will keep for up to 1 week in the refrigerator.

SERVES 1

Old Square

Ice cubes

1 ounce cognac, such as Landy

1 ounce rye whiskey, such as Bulleit

1 ounce sweet vermouth, such as Dolin Rouge

¾ ounce Bénédictine

¼ teaspoon Angostura bitters

¼ teaspoon Peychaud's bitters

Orange twist, for garnish

Fill a rocks glass with ice cubes and chill in the refrigerator. Fill a cocktail shaker with ice cubes and add the cognac, whiskey, vermouth, Bénédictine, and both bitters. Use a tall spoon to stir the ingredients together. Strain the mixture into the chilled rocks glass. Garnish with the orange twist and serve.

SMOKY HOT SAUCE

MAKES ABOUT 3 CUPS

Sriracha is a very popular hot sauce used in a lot of Asian dishes. Chefs in America have grown addicted to this spicy paste and put it on just about everything from pizza to pork chops. Another popular way to use it is to mix it with mayonnaise and serve it with crispy goodies. We made our own version of this sauce using our homemade hot sauce. Serve this with Fried Okra (page 99) or any other dipping food, such as hot wings. ★ C.G.

2 cups mayonnaise

½ cup Hot Sauce (page 28) or store-bought

1 tablespoon liquid smoke

1 tablespoon Old Bay Seasoning

1 tablespoon sugar

¼ teaspoon cayenne pepper

2 cloves garlic, finely minced or pressed through a garlic press

Kosher salt and freshly ground black pepper

Place the mayonnaise, hot sauce, liquid smoke, Old Bay, sugar, cayenne, and garlic in a medium bowl and mix well. Season with salt and pepper to taste. Place in an airtight container and refrigerate until ready to serve. It will keep for up to 1 week in the refrigerator.

SAUERKRAUT SAUCE

This is an American version of a French sauce called *gribiche*. It's creamy and gets a great sour kick from the sauerkraut. This pairs especially well with Fried Green Tomatoes (page 98), but it is also delicious with the Fried Okra or Crispy Fried Eggplant (page 99 or 101) or on the Cornmeal-Fried Catfish (page 94). It's great with cured meats and fish too. ★ C.G.

2 cups mayonnaise

¼ cup sauerkraut, drained

2 pickled cherry peppers

2 tablespoons whole-grain mustard

1 tablespoon celery seeds

2 cloves garlic, smashed

1 teaspoon ground mustard

1 bunch flat-leaf parsley, stemmed and chopped

Juice of 2 lemons

Salt and freshly ground black pepper

Place the mayonnaise, sauerkraut, cherry peppers, whole-grain mustard, celery seeds, garlic, ground mustard, parsley, and lemon juice in a food processor fitted with a metal blade. Puree until smooth. Season with salt and pepper to taste. Transfer the sauce to an airtight container and refrigerate until ready to serve. It will keep for up to 1 week in the refrigerator.

SIX

Baked and Sweet

In my childhood home, you could always find a tin of cookies on the counter or a pan of half-devoured brownies somewhere in the house. My mom was amazing about baking cookies for no reason, often at night after supper. My dad's eyes would light up when he would hear the unmistakable sound of mom's old Sunbeam mixer spinning, and my brother and I would each get a beater to lick.

My family comes from a long line of sweet-toothed people. My grandmother Frances put brown sugar in everything she baked and much of what she cooked; my grandmother Mary taught me how to enjoy a perfect cup of tea with sugar and milk, the way her English mother did. Today I continue the tradition of baking with my children and reliving those just-because moments. Just because we have butterscotch chips, we need to make something sweet tonight.

This chapter gathers together a collection of my favorite American recipes. Some have been passed down through our family, such as Irma's Chocolate Chip Cookies (page 134) and Parker House Rolls (page 109). Others have been tweaked over time in my own bakeshop, such as MOKan Nut Pie (page 118) and Oatmeal-Cherry Cookies (page 131). I often dream up desserts inspired by childhood nostalgia—I remember the small-town ice cream shops we visited on family vacations, the many state fairs and summer carnivals I attended and the sweet fried dough we would wait in long lines for, and afternoons spent standing high on a ladder in our yard with my mom's big lime green Tupperware container, collecting sour cherries to later pit and bake into a perfect cherry pie.

Family and food create memories in our home, maybe desserts most of all. ★ M.G.

At Thanksgiving and Christmas, you will find my mother-in-law, Kristie, on our doorstep, bundled up for a chilly day and holding a pan of her freshly baked rolls as she arrives to celebrate the day with us. For years I have admired her beautiful Parker House rolls stacked tall on a platter. Before opening our second restaurant, Rye, in Kansas, I asked Kristie if we could use her recipe to make our table bread. And just as Kristie shared it with me, I now share with you this wonderfully simple recipe for delicious yeast-raised rolls. Place the freshly baked rolls in a basket and serve with butter and Strawberry, Lemon, and Thyme Jam (page 32) alongside. ★ M.G.

¾ cup warm water

1 tablespoon active dry yeast

4 cups unbleached all-purpose flour

¾ cup whole milk, at room temperature

⅓ cup sugar

2 large eggs, lightly beaten

1 tablespoon kosher salt

⅓ cup shortening

Melted unsalted butter, for brushing rolls

PARKER HOUSE ROLLS

Grease two baking sheets with shortening and set aside.

In the bowl of a stand mixer, combine the warm water and yeast and mix with a fork to dissolve the yeast. Add the flour, milk, sugar, eggs, salt, and shortening. Using the dough hook attachment, mix on medium speed until the dough comes together, about 6 minutes. Turn the dough onto a floured surface and knead until the dough is smooth. Grease a large bowl and place the dough inside; cover lightly with a dry cloth and set in a warm place until the dough has doubled in size, about 2 hours.

Once the dough has doubled, punch the dough down and turn out onto a lightly floured work surface. Divide the dough into 24 pieces weighing 1⅔ ounces each. Cup your palm around one dough piece on the work surface and, with your fingers closed tightly around the dough, roll the piece into a ball. Place the ball onto one greased baking sheet. Repeat with the remaining pieces of dough. Place the baking sheet uncovered in a warm place once again until the rolls have doubled in size, 20 to 30 minutes.

Meanwhile, preheat the oven to 400°F. Once the rolls have doubled in size, carefully brush the tops with the melted butter. Bake the rolls until golden brown, 12 to 15 minutes. Allow the rolls to cool to room temperature in the pans before turning out. These rolls can be served at room temperature or rewarmed in a 200°F oven if needed, but they should be baked and eaten the same day. Leftover rolls may be frozen in a resealable plastic bag for up to 1 month and used later for a bread pudding or casserole.

CORN BREAD MUFFINS

Makes 24 muffins

Tell me the part of the country you're from and I'll tell you how you like your corn bread. Southerners, for example, have their own way—keep it simple, more savory, less sweet—and we in the Midwest have ours. Corn bread with whole corn kernels and a touch of sugar is the kind I know and love. When I was growing up, corn bread was always on our table, served with chili, ham-and-bean stews, pork chops, and even with fancy meals and on holidays. This is a quick bread that can make a baker out of anyone—if you can measure and stir, then you can make a mean corn bread. If you prefer, you can make this in a 9 by 13-inch pan; bake it for the same amount of time. ★ M.G.

1¾ cups yellow cornmeal

1¼ cups unbleached all-purpose flour

¾ cup sugar

1½ tablespoons baking powder

2 teaspoons kosher salt

1½ cups whole milk

8 tablespoons (1 stick) unsalted butter, melted

2 large eggs

1 cup fresh corn kernels

¼ cup chopped scallions

Preheat the oven to 350°F. Spray two 12-cup muffin pans with nonstick cooking spray and set aside.

In a large bowl, whisk the cornmeal, flour, sugar, baking powder, and salt to combine. In a medium bowl, whisk the milk, melted butter, and eggs until smooth. Add the butter mixture to the dry ingredients and mix just to combine. Fold the corn and scallions into the batter.

Scoop the batter into the prepared muffin tins, filling the tins three-quarters full. Bake until the corn bread is lightly golden, about 15 minutes.

Gently tap the pan to remove the baked muffins; let cool to room temperature. Serve immediately, or store in an airtight container for no more than 1 day. Corn bread muffins are best made and eaten on the same day.

LEMON MERINGUE PIE

★ ★ ★ ★ ★ ★ ★

MAKES ONE 9-INCH PIE

Finely grated zest and juice of
  6 lemons

6 large eggs

10 large egg yolks

2 cups sugar, divided

1 cup (2 sticks) unsalted butter,
  softened

1 teaspoon kosher salt

1 blind-baked Classic Piecrust
  (recipe follows)

½ cup egg whites (3 large whites)

SPECIAL EQUIPMENT

Handheld kitchen torch

Piping bag

The lemon meringue pie is not for everyone, but if you like a super rich, tart, puckery filling, then this is the recipe for you. The meringue topping is sweet and creamy, following my tried-and-true rule: Use a 2-to-1 sugar–to–egg whites ratio, and you will have a fantastic, glossy meringue. And if you get enough torch on the meringue, you will add a little of that wonderful campfire-toasted flavor. I particularly enjoy this pie in the winter, when it adds a bright flavor to a normally dreary time of year. You can also substitute Meyer lemons during the late winter months when they are in season. Meyer lemons will add a floral scent to this pie and make for a slightly softer lemon flavor. ★ M.G.

Preheat the oven to 375°F.

Fill a medium saucepan two-thirds full with water. In a large nonreactive bowl (see Note, page 112) whisk the lemon zest, lemon juice, eggs, egg yolks, and 1 cup of the sugar to combine. Place the bowl over the sauce pan to create a double boiler (do not let the bottom of the bowl touch the water). Heat the pot over medium heat and whisk the contents of the bowl constantly until the mixture thickens to a pudding consistency, about 12 minutes.

Once the mixture is thick, remove the bowl from the heat and quickly strain the lemon curd through a fine-mesh sieve to remove any cooked egg particles. While the lemon curd is still hot, whisk in the softened butter and salt. Spread the prepared filling into the blind-baked piecrust and bake just until the filling is set, 15 to 20 minutes. Remove the pie from the oven and let cool to room temperature.

Meanwhile, to make the meringue, combine the egg whites and the remaining 1 cup sugar in the clean bowl of an electric mixer. Place the bowl over the saucepan on the stove to make another double boiler (do not let the bottom of the bowl touch the water). With the saucepan over medium heat, whisk the egg whites and sugar in the bowl just until the sugar granules have dissolved, 8 to 10 minutes, being careful not to cook the egg whites around the edges. Remove the mixer bowl from the heat and return the bowl to the mixer. Using the whip attachment, whip the egg whites and sugar on high speed until a light, fluffy meringue forms (medium peaks). Set aside for use on the baked pie, up to 1 hour.

Continued

When the pie has cooled to room temperature, use a piping bag fitted with a plain wide tip to pipe the whipped meringue in dollops onto the filling, starting in the center of the pie and working outward in circles until the entire top of the pie is covered with meringue. With a handheld kitchen torch, lightly toast the top of the meringue. Alternatively, brown the meringue in the oven under the broiler, 1 minute or less. Chill the pie uncovered until ready to serve, but be sure to serve the pie the same day. Any leftovers can be refrigerated uncovered.

 NOTE **Certain recipes call for nonreactive bowls (or other cookware) because many foods—especially salty or acidic ones—react with untreated surfaces such as copper and aluminum. When the foods react, the metals dissolve, and the foods pick up a metallic taste, according to Harold McGee, author of *On Food and Cooking: The Science and Lore of the Kitchen*. Stainless-steel, glass, or ceramic bowls are the best nonreactive choices.**

Classic Piecrust Makes one 9-inch double crust or two 9-inch single crusts

The piecrust: It scares some, but it was my favorite pastry to master. In my early days in the bakeshop, I always had so much fun mixing, kneading, and rolling out the dough—even if the crust did not turn out right! This recipe was developed over time and through many attempts to find the right balance between good butter flavor and the delicate texture that lard creates, plus the perfect mix of sugar and salt. With very few ingredients in a crust, it's important to use the highest quality ingredients possible. I recommend using a good-quality butter that's high in butterfat, such as Plugra, to ensure that the crust will form properly, and a delicate salt like kosher or sea salt. Remember: Making pie is not easy, and there is no bakeshop secret to becoming a great pie maker. Patience and practice are the keys.

2⅓ cups unbleached all-purpose flour

1 tablespoon sugar

¾ teaspoon kosher salt

8 tablespoons (1 stick) cold unsalted butter, cubed

½ cup cold lard, cubed

½ cup ice water

1 large egg, lightly beaten

Combine the flour, sugar, and salt in the bowl of a food processor and set in the freezer for 30 minutes; you want all the components to be very cold in order to get the flakiest crust possible. Place the cubed butter and lard on a baking sheet and set in the freezer to chill until hard.

Continued

Attach the bowl with the dry ingredients to the food processor. Add the cold butter and lard to the dry ingredients in two additions, pulsing to combine after each addition. Slowly add the ice water to the mixture, pulsing to combine until a dough forms. As soon as the dough holds together in the food processor, quickly transfer the dough to a cold work surface. Knead the dough just until smooth, working the fat into streaks and being careful not to overwork the pie dough. Divide the dough in half and flatten each piece into a disk. Wrap the disks in plastic wrap and refrigerate for at least 2 hours or preferably overnight.

To form the crust, dust a work surface and the rolling pin with flour. Place one dough disk on the floured work surface and press the dough down in the center with the palm of your hand to flatten slightly. Then pound the dough flat with the rolling pin. Roll the dough in one full pass, then rotate the dough a few inches and roll again. Continue rotating the dough and rolling, dusting slightly with flour only if needed, until the dough is large enough to fit the pie dish and is about 1/8 inch thick. Gently cut the dough to the desired pan size using a pot lid or bowl as a guide. Gently slide both hands under the dough and hold the dough with the bottom side of your hands and forearms. Quickly slide the dough into the pie pan and gently press the dough into the pan. Crimp the pie dough around the edge and set in the freezer for at least 30 minutes before proceeding. The pie crusts can be kept frozen in the pie pans (or in a disk for the top crust), each double-wrapped in plastic, for up to 1 month.

To blind-bake (bake the crust before adding the pie filling), preheat the oven to 375°F. Line the frozen shell with a coffee filter and fill the liner with pie weights or uncooked pinto beans. Press the beans lightly into the shell to ensure that the edges are weighed down. Bake for 20 minutes, rotating 180 degrees halfway through the cooking time, until the outer edge of the crimp looks dry and golden brown. Remove the shell from the oven and carefully remove the coffee liner and beans. If the liner sticks to the shell, return the shell to the oven to dry out for about 3 minutes and then try to remove the liner. Decrease the oven temperature to 350°F. Brush the crimped edge and the bottom of the shell with the beaten egg and then prick the bottom of the shell. Return the shell to the oven and continue to bake until golden brown, 8 to 10 minutes longer. Set the baked shell aside until needed for final pie preparation.

BANANA CREAM PIE

MAKES ONE 9-INCH PIE

1 blind-baked Classic Piecrust (page 112)

½ cup bittersweet chocolate chips, melted

2 cups whole milk

1 vanilla bean, split and scraped

1 teaspoon pure vanilla extract

½ cup sugar

¼ cup cornstarch, sifted

4 large egg yolks

½ teaspoon kosher salt

4 tablespoons (½ stick) unsalted butter, softened

3 very ripe bananas, sliced about ⅛ inch thick

1½ cups heavy cream

½ cup ground Salted Toffee (page 97)

On chilly winter nights, my mom would sometimes whip up a batch of warm vanilla or butterscotch pudding and top it with Nilla Wafers and sliced ripe bananas. She would often serve these perfect puddings in little glass ramekins, which made dinner seem very fancy. Now at home with my little ones, I always make sure we have a box of Nilla Wafers in the pantry, as you never know when pudding, bananas, and Nillas will be needed as a treat! My recipe for banana cream pie is an ode to the creamy banana memories of my childhood. I coat the pie shell with a thin layer of dark chocolate to help the crust stay crispy under the pastry cream. If you prefer, a graham cracker crust can be substituted for the traditional piecrust here. ★ M.G.

Using a pastry brush, evenly coat the bottom and sides of the blind-baked piecrust with the melted chocolate, and set the crust in the refrigerator to set the chocolate.

In a medium sauce pan, heat the milk, vanilla bean and seeds, and vanilla extract over medium heat for about 3 minutes to bring the mixture to just below boiling. Meanwhile, in a large bowl, whisk together the sugar, cornstarch, egg yolks, and salt. Slowly whisk the hot milk into the cornstarch mixture in thirds so as not to curdle the egg yolks. Return the entire mixture to the sauce pan and whisk constantly until the pastry cream is thick, about 4 minutes. Whisk in the softened butter. Remove the pastry cream from the stovetop and discard the vanilla bean pod. Fold in the sliced bananas. Transfer the pastry cream to a bowl and cover with plastic wrap, pressing the wrap directly onto the pastry cream surface. Chill the pastry cream for about 30 minutes so that it is cool enough not to melt the chocolate when it is added to the crust.

Once the pastry cream is cool, fill the prepared piecrust and cover the top with plastic wrap, pressing it directly onto the pastry cream surface. Chill for at least 1 hour or overnight.

To serve, whip the heavy cream until stiff peaks form. Slice the pie into even slices, dollop each slice with whipped cream, and sprinkle the pie slices with ground salted toffee. Alternatively, if taking the pie to an event or for a dramatic presentation, top the entire pie with the whipped cream and ground salted toffee. The pie will keep in the refrigerator for up to 3 days.

MOKAN Nut Pie

★ ★ ★ ★ ★ ★ ★

MAKES ONE 9-INCH PIE

This is my Missouri-Kansas version of the classic pecan pie. Pecans are typically found in southern regions, but sometimes you find pecans in the north if the soil is rich enough. On our family farm in Parker, Kansas, we have a large pecan tree. The original farmhouse, dating to the 1800s, was destroyed by a tornado, but the pecan tree survived Mother Nature's wrath, and in early September the ground in front of the old 1903 farmhouse is dotted with small, rich pecans. I imagine the original owners gathering these precious nuts and making the most delicious pecan pies. That thought inspired this pie, for which I use local Missouri pecans (which are larger and easier to shell than our family pecans) and Kansas black walnuts, folded into a sweet bourbon filling. You can make this pie with only one kind of nut, but the mix of the two is truly outstanding. ★ M.G.

10 tablespoons (1¼ sticks) unsalted butter
6 large eggs
1 cup granulated sugar
1 cup Steen's cane syrup (see Note)
2½ tablespoons bourbon
2 teaspoons kosher salt
1 teaspoon pure vanilla extract
1½ cups chopped and toasted Missouri pecans (or your favorite pecans)
1½ cups chopped and toasted Kansas black walnuts (or your favorite walnuts)
1 blind-baked Classic Piecrust (page 112)
1½ cups heavy cream
Confectioners' sugar, for dusting

Melt the butter in a medium sauce pan over medium heat. Decrease the heat to medium-low and slowly cook until the butter begins to foam. Once the foam subsides, watch the butter carefully; it should start to toast and give off a nutty scent after about 6 minutes. When the butter has browned (you will notice little dark specks in the butter), remove the pot from the heat. The brown butter will be extremely hot at this point, so handle carefully. Allow the brown butter to cool to room temperature.

Strain the cooled brown butter through a fine-mesh sieve lined with a coffee filter into a clean, dry medium bowl (if your bowl has any water or moisture in it, it will cause the brown butter to spatter). You should now have about ½ cup of clarified brown butter. Reserve at room temperature for making the pie filling or keep chilled in an airtight container for up to 1 month. Bring to room temperature before continuing.

Preheat the oven to 350°F. In a large bowl, whisk together the eggs, granulated sugar, cane syrup, bourbon, salt, vanilla, and the brown butter. Stir in both nuts. Pour the prepared filling into the blind-baked piecrust and bake until the filling is set, about 45 minutes. Let cool to room temperature. When ready to serve, whip the heavy cream until soft peaks form. Serve each slice with a dollop of whipped cream and a dusting of confectioners' sugar. This pie may be kept at room temperature for 2 days or refrigerated for up to 1 week.

Steen's 100% Pure Cane Syrup is a Southern and Midwest pantry staple. It's available at many grocery and specialty stores, and online at steensyrup.com. You can substitute dark corn syrup, if necessary, but pure cane syrup is definitely better.

Lemon Cake
WITH WHITE CHOCOLATE
BUTTERCREAM

10 tablespoons (1¼ sticks) unsalted butter, softened
2¼ cups sugar
Finely grated zest and juice of 2 lemons (about ⅓ cup juice)
1 teaspoon pure vanilla extract
3 cups cake flour
1 tablespoon baking powder
¼ teaspoon kosher salt
1¾ cups water
¾ cup egg whites (4 large whites)
Lemon Cream (recipe follows)
White Chocolate Buttercream (recipe follows)

Preheat the oven to 350°F. Butter the sides and bottom of a 10-inch round springform cake pan and set aside.

In the bowl of a stand mixer fitted with the paddle attachment, cream the butter with 1¼ cups of the sugar until light and fluffy, about 8 minutes. Add the lemon zest, lemon juice, and vanilla and mix for 3 minutes to incorporate.

Whisk together the cake flour and baking powder in a medium bowl. Pass through a fine-mesh sieve two times. Sprinkle the salt over the sifted flour mixture. Add the sifted dry ingredients alternately with the water into the creamed butter mixture in two additions, scraping the sides of the bowl after each addition. Transfer the butter mixture to a large bowl and set aside.

In the bowl of a stand mixer fitted with the whip attachment, whip the egg whites until frothy. Once the egg whites begin to froth, slowly stream in the remaining 1 cup sugar, then whip on high speed until a meringue forms with medium peaks. Fold the whipped egg whites into the butter-flour mixture.

Continued

MAKES ONE
10-INCH CAKE

This cake is adapted from a recipe handed down to me that was called "The Ultimate White Cake." Naturally, when I read the title, I had to test it to see if it lived up to the name. And indeed, it is wonderful, with a rich lemon flavor and a lot of butter, but a very light texture. It's become my go-to cake for special occasions, particularly for spring events like Easter or Mother's Day. This recipe is also very versatile: You can swap out the lemon zest and juice for other flavorings such as pistachio paste, almond flavoring, or even passion fruit purée, to name just a few I've tried. For best results, the preparation of this cake should be a 3-day process: Make the lemon cream and buttercream on day 1; bake, fill, and freeze the cake on day 2; then frost and serve on day 3. The cake can also be made 1 week in advance—wrap and store the filled cake in the freezer until ready to frost with the buttercream and serve. Allow the cake to defrost overnight in the refrigerator before icing to prevent condensation. ★ M.G.

Pour the cake batter into the prepared cake pan to fill about three-quarters full (discard any remaining batter). Bake until the cake is domed in shape and a light golden color and a toothpick inserted into the center of the cake comes out clean, about 1 hour. Let the cake cool to room temperature before removing it from the pan.

To remove the cake from the pan, carefully run a knife around the edge of the pan and invert the pan onto a platter. Release the sides of the pan and carefully lift off the bottom of the pan. Use a bread knife to slice the cake horizontally into three even layers.

To assemble the layer cake, spread half of the chilled lemon cream on the bottom cake layer. Top with the second cake layer and spread the rest of the lemon cream on top. Top with the third cake layer. Wrap the cake with plastic wrap, and freeze for 1 hour or preferably overnight for best results.

Have the buttercream at room temperature for frosting. Transfer about 1 cup of the buttercream to a piping bag with a wide plain tip. Use the remaining buttercream frosting to evenly frost the top and sides of the cake. Finish with a simple piped bead around the base of the cake. Chill until serving.

Lemon Cream **Makes 3 cups**

Lemon cream is a staple in my pastry kitchen. I think of it the way a savory chef thinks of a mother sauce. Fresh lemon curd—or cream, as I call it here, since it has a higher butter content than a normal lemon curd—is incredibly versatile. Besides filling cakes with it, I serve this with freshly baked scones, biscuits, and muffins. It is also wonderful dolloped over summer berries or layered between shortbread. This lemon cream can also be stored in the freezer for up to 2 weeks if needed; but the fresher, the better.

5 large eggs

1 cup sugar

Finely grated zest of 1 lemon

Juice of 5 lemons (about ¾ cup)

18 tablespoons (2¼ sticks) unsalted butter, softened

Fill a large bowl with ice and set aside.

Fill a medium sauce pan two-thirds full with water. Place the eggs, sugar, lemon zest, and lemon juice in a nonreactive bowl (see Note, page 112). Place the bowl over the sauce pan to create a double boiler (do not let the bottom of the bowl touch the water). Heat the sauce pan over medium heat and whisk the egg mixture in the bowl constantly until the lemon cream thickens to resemble a loose pudding, about 12 minutes. Whisk in the softened butter 1 tablespoon at a time, making sure the butter is completely melted and combined after each addition.

Strain the lemon cream through a fine-mesh sieve into a bowl and place in the ice bath to cool quickly. Place plastic wrap directly onto the surface of the lemon cream to prevent a skin from forming. Allow the lemon cream to chill completely and set; keep refrigerated until needed for filling the lemon cake, up to 1 week.

White Chocolate Buttercream   Makes 2½ cups

I use this buttercream recipe for almost anything I frost, from cakes to sandwich cookies. This buttercream is a Swiss meringue style, which simply means the egg whites and sugar are heated together first over a double boiler to dissolve the sugar before whipping and adding the butter. The meringue is also wonderful on its own if you leave out the butter and flavorings. This recipe includes white chocolate, which helps to round out the creamy flavor and gives it an off-white color. You can also leave out the white chocolate if you prefer, or use melted dark chocolate for a chocolate buttercream, or add additional flavoring extracts or food coloring, depending on your final creation.

½ cup egg whites (3 large whites)

1 cup sugar

1½ cups (3 sticks) unsalted butter, softened

½ teaspoon pure vanilla extract

Pinch of kosher salt

⅛ cup chopped white chocolate or small white chocolate chips, melted

Fill a large sauce pan two-thirds full with water and set over medium heat.

In the bowl of a stand mixer, combine the egg whites and sugar and set over the sauce pan (do not let the bottom of the bowl touch the water). Whisk the egg whites and sugar constantly until the sugar is dissolved, about 8 minutes.

Transfer the bowl to the stand mixer; using the whip attachment, whip the egg whites and sugar on high speed until a stiff meringue forms, about 5 minutes. Once the meringue whips up, lower the mixer speed to medium and add the softened butter to the meringue. The meringue will break down slightly and look broken after adding all the butter, but keep mixing: The buttercream will whip up and turn soft and silky after about 3 minutes. Once the buttercream is whipped, add the vanilla, salt, and white chocolate and mix until combined.

Use the buttercream while soft to frost the filled lemon cake, or transfer to an airtight container and keep chilled for up to 1 week. Allow the buttercream to soften to room temperature, then re-whip on high speed using the paddle attachment until soft and creamy.

Spicy Ginger Cake

Aromatic, pungent, and spicy, fresh ginger adds a special flavor to baked foods—and it's readily available year-round in the produce section of your local market. We think of a typical ginger cake as dark and rich, filled with winter spices and blackstrap molasses. But I've created a lighter cake, with more emphasis on the fresh, natural gingerroot. I usually grate the gingerroot straight into the batter to make sure that all the ginger juices do not end up on the chopping board, so I tend to eyeball the grated ginger measurement. This cake has no season: It would be great in the spring or summer with fresh mint and berries, or perfect on a winter night with caramelized apples or poached quince. This cake will also bake well in a loaf pan or cupcake molds, if you prefer; just be aware that it will bake faster in cupcake molds, so make sure to watch it carefully. ★ M.G.

1¼ cups (2½ sticks) unsalted butter, softened

1⅓ cups firmly packed light brown sugar

⅔ cup granulated sugar

2 tablespoons peeled and grated fresh ginger

4 large eggs

2½ cups unbleached all-purpose flour

1½ teaspoons baking powder

1½ teaspoons baking soda

1 teaspoon salt

½ teaspoon ground allspice

2 cups buttermilk

Cream Cheese Frosting (recipe follows)

Preheat the oven to 350°F. Butter a 9-inch round cake pan and set aside.

In the bowl of a stand mixer fitted with the paddle attachment, cream the butter and both sugars until very light and fluffy, about 4 minutes. Add the grated ginger and mix for 1 more minute. Scrape down the bowl and add the eggs one at a time, mixing after each addition. Whisk together the flour, baking powder, baking soda, salt, and allspice. Alternately add the flour mixture and the buttermilk to the batter in two additions, scraping and mixing well, as the batter will appear broken from the ginger and buttermilk.

Pour the batter into the prepared pan and smooth the top. Bake until lightly golden brown and a toothpick inserted in the center comes out clean, about 55 minutes. Let the cake cool in the pan for about 10 minutes, then invert onto a plate. Let the cake cool to room temperature before frosting.

To frost, cut the cake in half horizontally using a serrated knife. Place the bottom layer on a cake stand. Spoon about ½ cup of cream cheese frosting onto the cake layer and evenly spread just until it reaches the edges of the cakes. Top the bottom layer with the second layer and press down evenly. Spoon the remainder of the frosting on top of the cake and evenly frost the top and sides of the cake. Transfer the cake to the refrigerator and chill until serving.

Cream Cheese Frosting ᴹᵃᵏᵉˢ 2 ᶜᵘᵖˢ

Tangy and sweet, this classic cream cheese frosting can be piped or smeared onto cake tops to add the finishing touch. This recipe has grated fresh ginger mixed in, but it can be omitted if you prefer a plain frosting—or add brandy or bourbon along with toasted nuts. ★ M.G.

16 ounces cream cheese, softened

1 cup (2 sticks) unsalted butter, cut into pieces, softened

3 cups confectioners' sugar

2 teaspoons pure vanilla extract

1 tablespoon peeled and grated fresh ginger

In the bowl of a stand mixer fitted with the paddle attachment, beat the cream cheese until soft and smooth, about 5 minutes. Gradually add the butter and continue beating until smooth and well blended, about 2 minutes longer. Sift the sugar into the mixture, and continue beating until smooth, about 2 minutes. Add the vanilla and ginger and stir to combine. Keep the frosting at room temperature until ready to frost, or transfer to an airtight container and keep chilled for up to 2 weeks. Let soften at room temperature before using.

PEACH BUCKLE

★ ★ ★ ★ ★ ★ ★

SERVES 6 TO 8

The buckle—a relative of the brown Betty and the cobbler is an old-fashioned single layer cake with fruit woven throughout and a crunchy nut or streusel topping. The cake batter "buckles" around the fruit as it bakes, giving this dessert its vintage name. This simple cake is a perfect excuse to use fresh or preserved summer fruit. This recipe calls for peaches; however, nectarines, blueberries, or sour cherries would also work wonderfully in this brandy-perfumed cake. I love serving this cake warm from the oven with only a dusting of confectioners' sugar, but fresh whipped cream or ice cream would of course be delicious additions. Serve this at a summer barbecue —or for breakfast! ★ M.G.

1½ cups cake flour
1½ teaspoons baking powder
½ teaspoon kosher salt
3 large eggs
5 large egg yolks
1½ cups plus 2 tablespoons granulated sugar
3 tablespoons peach juice (or orange juice)
2 tablespoons brandy
1 teaspoon pure vanilla extract
¾ cup (1½ sticks) unsalted butter, melted
1 pound peaches, peeled, pitted, and cut into ½-inch pieces (3 cups)
½ teaspoon ground cardamom
½ cup sliced almonds
Confectioners' sugar, for dusting

Preheat the oven to 350°F. Butter four 6-inch cast-iron skillets or one 8 by 12-inch baking pan and set aside.

In a small bowl, sift together the cake flour and baking powder. Sprinkle the kosher salt over the sifted flour mixture. In a large bowl, whisk together the eggs, egg yolks, the 1½ cups granulated sugar, peach juice, brandy, and vanilla. Add the dry flour mixture in three additions to the wet egg mixture, mixing well after each addition. Add the melted butter to the cake batter. Fold in the peaches. Spread the batter into the prepared skillets or baking pan.

In a small bowl, mix together the remaining 2 tablespoons granulated sugar, cardamom, and almonds. Sprinkle the mixture over the top of the cake batter. Bake until a toothpick inserted into the center comes out clean and the topping is golden, about 30 minutes for the 6-inch skillets or 50 minutes for the large baking pan. Serve warm, dusted with confectioners' sugar.

CORN COOKIES
with
MILK JAM AND STRAWBERRIES

★ ★ ★ ★ ★ ★ ★ ★

MAKES 24 COOKIES or 12 sandwich cookies

Corn stalks tall and green lined the roadways in the summer when we traveled through the Midwest on family vacations, and family picnics with Grandma and Grandpa always included freshly cut Ohio corn when we visited my mom's hometown. Today, corn is one of my favorite flavors in pastries, as in this corn cookie, which can be enjoyed alone or sandwiched with Milk Jam (as we call *dulce de leche*) and fresh strawberries. The corn cookies can be made and baked on the same day, or the dough and Milk Jam can be prepared the day before, and the dough rolled and frozen and then baked and sandwiched on the second day. ★ M.G.

1 cup (2 sticks) unsalted butter, softened
1½ cups granulated sugar
1 large egg
1⅔ cups unbleached all-purpose flour
¾ cup yellow cornmeal
¼ cup yellow corn flour
1½ teaspoons kosher salt
¾ teaspoon baking powder
¼ teaspoon baking soda
½ cup white chocolate chips, finely chopped
1 cup Milk Jam (recipe follows)
½ cup thinly sliced fresh strawberries
Confectioners' sugar, for dusting

In the bowl of a stand mixer fitted with the paddle attachment, cream the butter and granulated sugar until light and fluffy, about 7 minutes. Add the egg and mix well.

In a large bowl, whisk to combine the all-purpose flour, cornmeal, corn flour, salt, baking powder, and baking soda for 1 minute. Add the dry mixture to the creamed butter in thirds, scraping the bottom of the bowl and mixing well after each addition. Fold in the white chocolate chips.

Form the cookie dough into a long log (8 to 10 inches long) and wrap tightly with plastic wrap. Freeze for 1 hour or up to 1 day.

Preheat the oven to 350°F. Slice the frozen cookie dough into 24 slices about ¼ inch thick and place on an ungreased baking sheet, at least 1 inch apart. Bake until the cookies are cooked through and slightly golden along the edges, 8 to 10 minutes. Transfer the cookies to a rack and let cool to room temperature.

To assemble the sandwich cookies, use a small offset spatula to smear a coating of the milk jam onto the bottom sides of all the corn cookies. Top the jam on 12 of the cookies with 3 or 4 strawberry slices each, then top with the other 12 cookies to make sandwiches. Lightly dust with confectioners' sugar, and serve immediately. Unsandwiched cookies will keep for up to 1 week in an airtight container at room temperature.

Continued

Milk Jam   Makes 1 cup

It is said that *dulce de leche* originated in Argentina in 1829; sometime after that, the French discovered it and began using it in their pastries and baked goods. The simple version we make here is a milk jam. As with any good jam recipe, there are many variations: Some recipes call for cream instead of milk or a combination of the two; some add baking soda to the milk to aid in the browning of the jam; others may add a flavoring like vanilla bean, tea, or even chocolate. I keep it simple and true to the flavor of the milk fat. That said, use the freshest whole milk you can find, and if your city has a good local dairy, grab a glass bottle of their delicious milk.

2 cups whole milk

1 cup sugar

Pinch of kosher salt

In a medium sauce pan over medium heat, bring the milk and sugar to a boil, stirring frequently to dissolve the sugar and taking care that milk doesn't boil over. Add the salt and decrease the heat to low. Simmer gently, whisking occasionally, until the milk is thick and measures a scant 1 cup, about 40 minutes. Transfer the jam to a heatproof jar; let cool, then cover and chill. The jam will keep refrigerated for up to 1 week.

Crispy, chewy, soft in the center—that's my idea of a perfect oatmeal cookie. This variation features sweet cherries mashed into the dough, but if you preserve your own summer cherries, sweet or tart, either will be delicious in this recipe. I like Amarena cherries best here. You can find them in jars or cans at specialty food stores; the sweet cherry syrup they're packed in is also wonderful brushed over morning muffins or used in Cherry Limeade (page 141). ★ M.G.

- ¾ cup unbleached all-purpose flour
- ½ cup whole wheat flour
- ½ teaspoon baking soda
- ½ teaspoon ground cinnamon
- ¼ teaspoon ground nutmeg
- ¼ teaspoon kosher salt
- 1 cup (2 sticks) unsalted butter, softened
- 1 cup granulated sugar
- ½ cup firmly packed light brown sugar
- 2 large eggs
- 2 teaspoons pure vanilla extract
- 2 cups old-fashioned rolled oats
- 1 cup Amarena sour cherries in syrup or brandied sour cherries in syrup, drained
- Turbinado sugar, for sprinkling

OATMEAL-CHERRY COOKIES
MAKES 24 COOKIES

Place a rack in the center of the oven and preheat the oven to 350°F.

In a large bowl, whisk both flours, baking soda, cinnamon, nutmeg, and salt for 1 minute to combine.

In the bowl of a stand mixer fitted with the paddle attachment, cream the butter and both sugars until light and fluffy, about 8 minutes. Add the eggs and vanilla and mix well to combine. Add the dry ingredients, mixing until combined. Add the oats and cherries and mix until the cherries are mashed slightly and combined throughout the cookie dough. Be sure to scrape the bottom of the bowl to ensure that all ingredients are incorporated.

Using a 2-ounce cookie scoop, place 8 dollops of cookie dough evenly spaced on each of 3 baking sheets. Lightly sprinkle the tops of the cookie dough with turbinado sugar until evenly coated. Bake the cookies in batches on the center rack until golden brown, 10 to 12 minutes, rotating the pans halfway through baking. Using a spatula, transfer the warm cookies to a rack to cool to room temperature. Store in an airtight container at room temperature for up to 5 days.

When I was little, I often made chocolate–peanut butter cookies using the recipe from the Hershey cookbook that still sits in my kitchen today, stained with butter and chocolate fingerprints. This is my grown-up version of my longtime favorite cookie, using butterscotch chips in place of peanut butter. These cookies are very rich and keep a perfect shape while baking, so it's a great go-to recipe for a holiday cookie exchange. I love these cookies the way they are, but you could substitute peanut butter chips for butterscotch if you prefer, or replace half the butterscotch chips with semi-sweet chocolate chips to make the cookies extra chocolaty. Demerara sugar, a coarse, light amber sugar with a wonderful crunch, is typically used for sprinkling on top of cookies. In this recipe, I cream the Demerara sugar right into the cookie dough for a crunchy center texture. Specialty stores such as Dean & DeLuca carry Demerara sugar, but if you can't find it, you can use light brown sugar instead. ★ M.G.

CHOCOLATE-BUTTERSCOTCH COOKIES

1¼ cups (2½ sticks) unsalted butter, softened
1 cup granulated sugar
¾ cup firmly packed dark brown sugar
¼ cup Demerara sugar
2 teaspoons pure vanilla extract
2 large eggs
½ teaspoon kosher salt
2 cups unbleached all-purpose flour
¾ cup Dutch-processed cocoa powder
1 teaspoon baking soda
2 cups butterscotch chips

Preheat the oven to 350°F. In the bowl of a stand mixer fitted with the paddle attachment, cream the butter, all three sugars, and vanilla on medium speed until fluffy, about 5 minutes. Mix in the eggs one at a time, then add the salt. In a medium bowl, whisk together the flour, cocoa powder, and baking soda. Add the dry ingredients in three additions to the creamed butter mixture; mix well after each addition. Stir in the butterscotch chips.

Drop the dough by tablespoonfuls onto ungreased baking sheets, 1 to 2 inches apart. Bake until the cookies are domed in shape and the surface has gone from glossy to matte, about 10 minutes. Let the cookies sit for 2 minutes on the baking sheets before transferring to racks to cool. Store at room temperature in an airtight container for up to 2 days.

IRMA'S CHOCOLATE CHIP COOKIES

MAKES 36 COOKIES

2 cups unbleached all-purpose flour

1 teaspoon baking soda

½ teaspoon kosher salt

8 tablespoons (1 stick) unsalted butter, softened

½ cup solid bacon fat (see Note)

1¼ cups firmly packed light brown sugar

¼ cup granulated sugar

2 large eggs

2 teaspoons pure vanilla extract

2 cups semisweet chocolate chips

1 cup chopped walnuts (optional)

My father-in-law, Greg Garrelts, rarely bakes, but one year he made his mother's cookies for our annual Fourth of July celebration on the family farm. Set on the stovetop in a brushed aluminum can was Irma Garrelts's secret cookie weapon: bacon fat. I would love to think that Irma was very trendy in her patterned apron, baking with bacon fat, since pork products are so in style these days. But back then, efficiency was key: Nothing went to waste. Greg remembers the tiny galley kitchen they had, her electric hand mixer buzzing away, and her wonderful cookies stacked tall in the bright red cookie jar shaped like an apple on the countertop. Sadly, I never got to meet Irma, but I can tell from her recipe for chocolate chip cookies that she and I would have enjoyed baking together. You can substitute another half stick of butter for the bacon fat, if you prefer a more traditional cookie flavor. ★ M.G.

Preheat the oven to 350°F. In a large bowl, mix together the flour, baking soda, and salt.

In the bowl of a stand mixer fitted with the paddle attachment, cream the butter, bacon fat, and both sugars until light and fluffy, about 6 minutes. Beat in the eggs one at a time, scraping down the sides after each addition, then add the vanilla. With the mixer on medium-low, slowly add the flour mixture, beating until just combined. Remove from the mixer and stir in the chocolate chips and the walnuts until just incorporated.

Drop the dough by tablespoonfuls onto baking sheets, 9 to a sheet. Bake until the edges and tops are lightly browned, about 11 minutes. Using a spatula, transfer the warm cookies to a rack to cool completely. Store the cookies in an airtight container at room temperature for up to 3 days.

You may need to reserve the bacon fat from a few batches of bacon before baking these cookies. For best results, strain the bacon fat while still fluid through a fine-mesh sieve lined with a coffee filter to remove solid particles. Store in an airtight container in the refrigerator.

Greg Garrelts says to avoid peppered bacon as it will give your cookies quite a kick!

Rye Cookies

Rye flour is typically used in bread recipes, particularly in German and other eastern European recipes. Pumpernickel bread is the first thing that comes to mind when I think of rye flour. But I also like to work with it in the pastry shop, using rye flour in place of all-purpose flour in cookies and cakes. Whole wheat and rye flours have a sweet, nutty taste that adds layers of flavor to bread, so why not to pastries? This chewy, cake-like cookie is scented with fresh orange zest and rolled in cinnamon sugar. My German Schultz ancestry shows through here: I bake these cookies as a nod to tradition and to the first Germans settlers in America. ★ M.G.

CINNAMON SUGAR

¼ cup granulated sugar

2¼ teaspoons ground cinnamon

½ teaspoon ground nutmeg

COOKIES

¾ cup (1½ sticks) unsalted butter

⅓ cup sour cream

3 large eggs

1 teaspoon pure vanilla extract

Finely grated zest of 1 orange

2 cups dark rye flour

1 cup unbleached all-purpose flour

1 cup granulated sugar

½ cup firmly packed dark brown sugar

1 teaspoon baking soda

½ teaspoon salt

½ teaspoon ground cinnamon

¼ teaspoon ground nutmeg

For the cinnamon sugar, combine the sugar, cinnamon, and nutmeg in a small bowl. Set aside until ready to use.

For the cookies, gently melt the butter in a small sauce pan over low heat or in the microwave. Let it cool slightly, then stir in the sour cream. Whisk the eggs into the cooled butter–sour cream mixture. Add the vanilla and the orange zest.

In a large bowl, stir together both flours, both sugars, and the baking soda, salt, cinnamon, and nutmeg.

Add the wet ingredients into the dry ingredients and stir just until the dough comes together. The cookie dough will be loose and very sticky once everything is incorporated. Chill the cookie dough in the freezer until it is firm enough to scoop and roll, about 30 minutes.

Meanwhile, preheat the oven to 350°F. Remove the dough from the freezer, scoop out a portion and roll into nine 1-inch balls, and roll them in the cinnamon sugar. Place the 9 balls on a baking sheet, and bake until the cookies are domed in shape, about 8 minutes. Keep the remaining dough in the freezer while baking the first batch so it remains firm enough to scoop. Let the baked cookies cool on the baking sheet for 5 minutes, then transfer to a rack to cool. Repeat with the remaining dough. Store the cookies at room temperature in an airtight container for up to 3 days.

BROWNIE AND PISTACHIO
ICE CREAM SANDWICH

MAKES 18 BROWNIES
OR 9 SANDWICHES

Oftentimes at dinner parties I will serve very simple desserts reminiscent of the things I loved as a kid—it's like asking my guests to relive their childhoods with me. I'll fancy up root beer floats with tall, pretty glasses and fun ice cream flavors, or I'll make ice cream sandwiches. Almost everyone loves a chocolate brownie, and when layered with homemade ice cream it is a truly irresistible dessert, especially in the summer. My mom originally found this brownie recipe and said we must try it—it appeared in a 1975 issue of *Ladies' Home Journal*, alongside an interview with Katharine Hepburn. We loved the chewy texture and the rich chocolate flavor of Ms. Hepburn's brownies. Here I revisit this beloved recipe with ice cream smashed between two layers of brownies for a wonderfully decadent ice cream sandwich. ★ M.G.

1 cup (2 sticks) unsalted butter

4 ounces unsweetened baking chocolate

2 cups sugar

4 large eggs, beaten

1 teaspoon pure vanilla extract

½ cup unbleached all-purpose flour

½ teaspoon kosher salt

2 cups chopped walnuts (or your favorite nut; optional)

Pistachio Ice Cream (recipe follows)

Preheat the oven to 350°F. Butter an 8 by 12-inch baking pan, line the pan with parchment paper, and butter it again. Set aside.

Fill a medium sauce pan two-thirds full with water and set over medium heat. Place the butter and chocolate in a medium bowl and set the bowl over the sauce pan (do not let the bottom of the bowl touch the water). Stir the butter and chocolate until melted. Remove the bowl from the heat and stir in the sugar. Add the eggs, vanilla, flour, and salt and stir until smooth. Fold in the nuts if using. Pour the batter into the prepared baking pan and smooth out the top. Bake until a toothpick inserted into the center comes out clean, 25 to 30 minutes.

Let the brownies cool to room temperature in the pan, and then transfer the pan to the freezer to chill for 1 hour. Invert the pan and tap the sides to remove the brownie from the pan. Carefully remove the parchment paper. Slice the chilled brownies into 18 squares and line them up a baking sheet lined with waxed paper. Place a medium scoop of ice cream onto half of the brownies and top with the other half of the brownies to make sandwiches. Freeze until firm before serving, about 2 hours.

Continued

Pistachio Ice Cream   Makes 1 quart

This ice cream can really be any flavor you want. The base recipe starts with egg yolks, heavy cream, milk, and sugar; I then add pistachio paste (available at specialty stores such as Dean & DeLuca), but you can use your imagination (see Note). No matter which flavoring you choose, I almost always recommend a pinch or so of salt, since salt in desserts has a wonderful way of balancing the sugar and making all the flavors pop, especially in ice cream. Never be afraid to add salt to dessert!

6 large egg yolks
2 cups heavy cream
1 cup whole milk
¾ cup sugar
⅛ teaspoon kosher salt
2 tablespoons pistachio paste

SPECIAL EQUIPMENT
Ice cream maker

Fill a large bowl with ice. Set aside.

Whisk the egg yolks in a medium bowl. In a large sauce pan over medium-high heat, bring the cream, milk, and sugar to a low simmer; simmer for 2 minutes, or until the sugar has fully dissolved. Watch the pot closely, as it can boil over quickly.

Temper the eggs by whisking 1 cup of the hot cream in a slow, steady stream into the yolks. You want to add the hot cream slowly to gradually increase the temperature of the egg yolks without scrambling them. Add the remainder of the cream to the eggs in the bowl. Strain the ice-cream base through a fine-mesh sieve into a large bowl. Whisk in the salt and pistachio paste.

Set the bowl inside the bowl with the ice and whisk the ice cream base until it has cooled slightly. Once the base has cooled, transfer it to an airtight container and refrigerate for at least 6 hours, or preferably overnight.

Churn the chilled base in an ice cream maker according to the manufacturer's instructions. Transfer the ice cream to a freezer-safe container. Freeze for at least 2 hours before serving.

For alternatives to the pistachio paste, try these flavorings.

Strawberry: Whisk in ¼ cup fresh strawberry purée after straining the ice cream base.
Peanut Butter: Whisk in ¼ cup peanut butter after straining the ice cream base.
Earl Grey Tea: Steep 1 Earl Grey tea bag along with the peel of 1 orange in the cream and milk as you heat them, about 10 minutes. Temper in the eggs and then strain the ice cream base through a fine mesh sieve after all the ingredients are added.

CHERRY LIMEADE

SERVES 6

1 cup pitted fresh Bing cherries, plus 6 pitted fresh Bing cherries for garnish

2 tablespoons dark cherry liqueur, such as Heering

8 to 10 fresh mint leaves, plus 6 sprigs mint for garnish

½ teaspoon freshly grated lime zest

¼ teaspoon vanilla bean paste

Lime Sorbet (recipe follows)

Cherry Soda (recipe follows)

1 lime, sliced ¼ inch thick, for garnish

I have fond childhood memories of summer nights spent in the local ice cream parlor in my hometown of Naperville, Illinois. The Oberweis dairy served ice cream in their stores and delivered milk to your doorstep. Just over the Washington Street Bridge was Cock-Robin, a family-owned ice cream place since 1931 and a time capsule, with amazing chocolate sodas, banana splits, and sugar cones stacked high with rainbow sherbet. This recipe is a tribute to those places—and a gift for Colby, my hubby, whose favorite frozen treat is the cherry limeade. This adult limeade features cherry liqueur, but you can use grenadine syrup for a kid-friendly version. I prefer fresh, sweet dark cherries to balance the tart lime sorbet, but frozen cherries will work, or sour cherries if you really want to pucker. To simplify this even further, you can use a purchased black cherry soda. ★ M.G.

In a medium bowl, combine the 1 cup cherries, cherry liqueur, mint leaves, lime zest, and vanilla bean paste. Using a muddler or the back of a wooden spoon, muddle the cherries and flavorings, pressing to combine and to release the oil in the mint leaves. Evenly distribute the cherry mash among 6 soda glasses. Using an ice cream scoop, place 2 scoops of the Lime Sorbet into each glass. Top with cherry soda and garnish each glass with a cherry, a lime slice, and a sprig of mint.

Lime Sorbet   Makes 1 quart

This sorbet can be served alone or in a float as in the Cherry Limeade. It also adapts well to many different variations. For a lemon-lime flavoring, replace half the lime juice with freshly squeezed lemon juice. Or use Key limes, which make a wonderful sorbet; they are more herbaceous than regular limes, and very tart. Sometimes I add buttermilk to my sorbet bases, and buttermilk-lime sorbet is a perfect combination: The tartness of the buttermilk pairs well with the lime, and the milk fat adds a creamy balance to the tart citrus. To do so, simply decrease the citrus juice by one-third and replace with buttermilk.

1½ cups freshly squeezed lime juice (about 10 limes)

1½ cups Simple Syrup (recipe follows)

1½ cups water

¼ cup light corn syrup

SPECIAL EQUIPMENT
Ice cream maker

In a large bowl, whisk the lime juice, simple syrup, water, and corn syrup to combine. Transfer the mixture to an ice cream maker and churn the mix according to the manufacturer's instructions (this may require chilling the base before churning). Transfer the sorbet to a freezer-safe container and freeze for at least 1 hour before serving. The sorbet will keep in the freezer for up to 1 month.

Continued

Simple Syrup   Makes 2 cups

Simple syrup is wonderful to have on hand for making sorbet, soaking cake layers, or using as a liquid sweetener for chilled beverages. Simple syrup also lends itself well to flavorings: Steep a fresh vanilla bean in it or infuse it with fresh herbs, such as lavender, thyme, or mint.

1½ cups sugar
1½ cups water

In a large sauce pan, whisk together the sugar and water. Bring the sugar water to a rapid boil over high heat. Decrease the heat to medium and simmer for 5 to 7 minutes, until the sugar is completely dissolved. Remove the syrup from the heat and let it cool to room temperature. Store the syrup in an airtight container in the refrigerator for up to 1 month.

Cherry Soda   Makes 4 cups

This cherry syrup, when charged in an iSi soda siphon, becomes a wonderfully rich and sweet dark cherry soda. The sweetened and reduced syrup can also be used in cocktails or to sweeten iced tea or other summer beverages.

3½ cups water
¼ cup sugar
3 tablespoons dark cherry syrup, such as Amarena cherry syrup

SPECIAL EQUIPMENT
iSi soda siphon and soda chargers

Combine the water, sugar, and cherry syrup in a medium sauce pan and bring to a boil over medium-high heat to dissolve the sugar. Remove the sauce pan from the heat and let the syrup cool slightly. Strain the hot syrup through a fine-mesh sieve. Pour the syrup into the iSi soda siphon, making sure not to exceed the fill line. Charge the iSi soda siphon according to the manufacturer's instructions and refrigerate for at least 2 hours. The Cherry Soda can be stored in the iSi container for up to 2 days. If the soda loses carbonation, you may have to recharge the iSi siphon with a new soda charger.

BUTTER MINTS

★ ★ ★ ★ ★ ★ ★

MAKES 15 DOZEN MINTS

My Grandma and Grandpa Freshley would drive 8 hours over snow-covered roads from Ohio to Illinois most every Christmas while I was little. We would greet them at the door with big hugs and kisses, and then Grandpa would unload the car, bringing in their pale blue luggage set and Grandma's mismatched cookie tins filled with her amazing collection of drop cookies, nut bars, and perfect pizzelle wafer cookies, all the layers separated with carefully cut sheets of waxed paper. Often she would make delicate little candies rolled in confectioners' sugar that were the quintessential handmade treat. These butter mints are my tribute to Grandma Freshley's holiday tin collection. Simply add peppermint and food coloring for a traditional candy or add cocoa powder for a chocolate variety—and if you can find cacao nibs at a specialty store, they add a delicious little bitter chocolate crunch to these soft mints. Like Grandma's candies, these mints, wrapped in waxed paper, are the perfect gift to share with friends and family. ★ M.G.

10 tablespoons (1¼ sticks) unsalted butter, softened
5 cups confectioners' sugar, plus more for dusting
⅓ cup sweetened condensed milk
1 teaspoon pure peppermint extract
½ teaspoon pure vanilla extract
½ teaspoon kosher salt
Gel food coloring in green and/or other colors (optional)
5 tablespoons high-quality unsweetened cocoa powder, such as Valrhona (optional)
1 tablespoon cocoa nibs, finely chopped (optional)

In the bowl of a stand mixer fitted with the paddle attachment, beat the butter on medium speed until smooth and free of lumps, about 5 minutes. Add the confectioners' sugar, sweetened condensed milk, both extracts, and salt. Mix everything together on low speed, and once the sugar is incorporated, increase the speed to medium and beat until the candy is nice and smooth.

You can leave the mints white or color them. For traditionally colored butter mints, drop the desired amount of green gel food coloring into the candy and mix to combine. You can also remove one-third to one-half of the candy mix to make different colors as well; just be sure to cover the reserved white candy mix with plastic wrap so it does not dry out while you're mixing the other portions. For chocolate butter mints, add the cocoa powder to the mix at the end and beat until smooth and completely incorporated. Add the chopped cocoa nibs and mix just until they are evenly distributed.

To shape the candy, dust a work surface with confectioners' sugar and line a baking sheet with waxed paper. Roll out the candy until it is about a ½-inch-thick rope, then use a sharp knife to cut small pieces, ½ to ¾ inch long. Transfer the pieces to a covered container, layering with wax paper, and repeat the rolling and cutting process if you have made different colors.

Store the butter mints in an airtight container in the refrigerator. Best kept chilled for up to 1 week.

HOLIDAY AND SPECIAL-EVENT MENUS

MOTHER'S DAY BRUNCH

Chipped Beef on Toast with Cured Beef and Spinach (page 4)

Blueberry-Oat Breakfast Cake (page 11)

Pimm's Punch (page 42)

CHILDREN'S BIRTHDAY

Garrelts Fried Chicken (page 91)

Parker House Rolls (page 109)

Cucumber-Dill Salad (page 46)

Lemon Cake with White Chocolate Buttercream (page 121)

Summer Picnic

BBQ Spareribs (page 79)

Quick Pickles (page 37)

Yukon Gold Potato Salad with Summer Corn, Country Ham, and Garlicky Lemon-Chive Dressing (page 45)

Honeyed Goat Cheese Spread (page 36) with toasted sourdough

Paloma Shrub (page 67)

BACK TO SCHOOL

Madeira-Braised Chicken with Sour Cherries (page 51)

Corn Bread Muffins (page 110)

Apple-Bourbon Butter (page 31)

Chocolate-Butterscotch Cookies (page 133)

AUTUMN SUPPER

Cider-Braised Brisket (page 60)

Corn Fritters with Fresh Sheep's Milk Cheese (page 21)

Dutch Oven–Roasted Carrots with Brown Sugar and Carrot Top Crumble (page 59)

MOKan Nut Pie (page 118)

Manhattan, Kansas (page 58)

RAINY DAY

Banana Cream Pie (page 116)

State Fair (page 96)

CHRISTMAS MORNING

Christmas Casserole (page 19)

Braised Bacon with Bourbon Raisins, Nuts, and Fried Eggs (page 22)

Fried Cinnamon Rolls (page 12)

Cranberry-Quince Preserves (page 35)

Bloody Mary (page 17)

METRIC CONVERSIONS AND EQUIVALENTS

METRIC CONVERSION FORMULAS

TO CONVERT	MULTIPLY
Ounces to grams	Ounces by 28.35
Pounds to kilograms	Pounds by .454
Teaspoons to milliliters	Teaspoons by 4.93
Tablespoons to milliliters	Tablespoons by 14.79
Fluid ounces to milliliters	Fluid ounces by 29.57
Cups to milliliters	Cups by 236.59
Cups to liters	Cups by .236
Pints to liters	Pints by .473
Quarts to liters	Quarts by .946
Gallons to liters	Gallons by 3.785
Inches to centimeters	Inches by 2.54

OVEN TEMPERATURES

To convert Fahrenheit to Celsius, subtract 32 from Fahrenheit, multiply the result by 5, then divide by 9.

Description	Fahrenheit	Celsius	British Gas Mark
Very cool	200°	95°	0
Very cool	225°	110°	1/4
Very cool	250°	120°	1/2
Cool	275°	135°	1
Cool	300°	150°	2
Warm	325°	165°	3
Moderate	350°	175°	4
Moderately hot	375°	190°	5
Fairly hot	400°	200°	6
Hot	425°	220°	7
Very hot	450°	230°	8
Very hot	475°	245°	9

COMMON INGREDIENTS AND THEIR APPROXIMATE EQUIVALENTS

1 cup uncooked white rice = 185 grams

1 cup all-purpose flour = 140 grams

1 stick butter (4 ounces • 1/2 cup • 8 tablespoons) = 110 grams

1 cup butter (8 ounces • 2 sticks • 16 tablespoons) = 220 grams

1 cup brown sugar, firmly packed = 225 grams

1 cup granulated sugar = 200 grams

Information compiled from a variety of sources, including Recipes into Type by Joan Whitman and Dolores Simon (Newton, MA: Biscuit Books, 1993); The New Food Lover's Companion by Sharon Tyler Herbst (Hauppauge, NY: Barron's, 2013); and Rosemary Brown's Big Kitchen Instruction Book (Kansas City, MO: Andrews McMeel, 1998).

APPROXIMATE METRIC EQUIVALENTS

VOLUME

1/4 teaspoon	1 milliliter
1/2 teaspoon	2.5 milliliters
3/4 teaspoon	4 milliliters
1 teaspoon	5 milliliters
1 1/4 teaspoons	6 milliliters
1 1/2 teaspoons	7.5 milliliters
1 3/4 teaspoons	8.5 milliliters
2 teaspoons	10 milliliters
1 tablespoon (1/2 fluid ounce)	15 milliliters
2 tablespoons (1 fluid ounce)	30 milliliters
1/4 cup	60 milliliters
1/3 cup	80 milliliters
1/2 cup (4 fluid ounces)	120 milliliters
2/3 cup	160 milliliters
3/4 cup	180 milliliters
1 cup (8 fluid ounces)	240 milliliters
1 1/4 cups	300 milliliters
1 1/2 cups (12 fluid ounces)	360 milliliters
1 2/3 cups	400 milliliters
2 cups (1 pint)	460 milliliters
3 cups	700 milliliters
4 cups (1 quart)	0.95 liter
1 quart plus 1/4 cup	1 liter
4 quarts (1 gallon)	3.8 liters

WEIGHT

1/4 ounce	7 grams
1/2 ounce	14 grams
3/4 ounce	21 grams
1 ounce	28 grams
1 1/4 ounces	35 grams
1 1/2 ounces	42.5 grams
1 2/3 ounces	45 grams
2 ounces	57 grams
3 ounces	85 grams
4 ounces (1/4 pound)	113 grams
5 ounces	142 grams
6 ounces	170 grams
7 ounces	198 grams
8 ounces (1/2 pound)	227 grams
16 ounces (1 pound)	454 grams
35.25 ounces (2.2 pounds)	1 kilogram

LENGTH

1/8 inch	3 millimeters
1/4 inch	6 millimeters
1/2 inch	1 1/4 centimeters
1 inch	2 1/2 centimeters
2 inches	5 centimeters
2 1/2 inches	6 centimeters
4 inches	10 centimeters
5 inches	13 centimeters
6 inches	15 1/4 centimeters
12 inches (1 foot)	30 centimeters

★ MADE IN AMERICA ★

Andrews McMeel Publishing, LLC,
an Andrews McMeel Universal company,
1130 Walnut Street, Kansas City, Missouri 64106

www.andrewsmcmeel.com

15 16 17 18 19 TEN 10 9 8 7 6 5 4 3 2 1

ISBN: 978-1-4494-5814-0

Library of Congress Control Number: 2014949610

DESIGN Holly Ogden
PHOTOGRAPHY Bonjwing Lee
EDITOR Jean Z. Lucas
ART DIRECTOR Tim Lynch
PRODUCTION EDITOR Maureen Sullivan
PRODUCTION MANAGER Cliff Koehler
DEMAND PLANNER Sue Eikos

WWW.BLUESTEMKC.COM
WWW.RYEKC.COM

ATTENTION: SCHOOLS AND BUSINESSES

Andrews McMeel books are available at quantity discounts with bulk purchase for educational, business, or sales promotional use. For information, please e-mail the Andrews McMeel Special Sales Department: specialsales@amuniversal.com